Recipe for a Cookbook

How to Write, Publish, and Promote Your Cookbook

Gloria Chadwick

Copper Canyon Books

Recipe for a Cookbook

Publisher's Cataloging-in-Publication Data

Chadwick, Gloria

Recipe for a Cookbook

1. Authorship 2. Food Writing I. Title

Library of Congress Control Number: 2008923571

ISBN 13: 978-1-883717-73-5
ISBN 10: 1-883717-73-6

Copper Canyon Books
10362 Sahara Street, Suite 1204
San Antonio, Texas 78216

www.chadwickpages.com

Please visit our website at
www.recipeforacookbook.com

Printed in the United States of America

Books by Gloria Chadwick

Discovering Your Past Lives
Spirituality & Self-Empowerment
Somewhere Over the Rainbow: A Soul's Journey Home
Reincarnation and Your Past-Life Memories
Magical Mind, Magical Life
The Key to Self-Empowerment
Soul Shimmers: Awakening Your Spiritual Self
Happy Ways to Heal the Earth
Life is Just a Dream
Parallel Lives: A Mystical Journey
Psychic Senses: How to Develop Your Innate Powers
Exploring Your Past Lives: A Workbook
Inner Journeys: Meditations and Visualizations
Future Lives: Discovering & Understanding Your Destiny
Who Were You? A Do-it-Yourself Guide to Past Life Regression
The Write Way: How to Write Your Book and Get it Published
The Path to Publishing Your Book
The Path to Self-Publishing
Zen Coffee

Cookbooks –

Really Good Recipes
Food Feasts
Best of the Barbecues
The Cheapie Chicken Cookbook
Foods & Flavors of San Antonio

This book is dedicated to you—the cookbook author.

Contents

This book is a guide that shows you how to create, cook, and serve your cookbook with style and flair. It offers food for thought by helping you become more knowledgeable about writing, publishing, and selling your cookbook; it provides plenty of know-how and generous portions of how-to for producing a cookbook. There are recipes to feed your imagination by showing various page layouts; they're also included in case you get hungry while reading this book or writing your cookbook.

Knowing the reasons why you want to write a cookbook will show you how to develop your cookbook's personality, influence how you write and market your cookbook, and help you find and target potential markets. How to clearly and thoroughly define the scope, theme, and focus of your cookbook. How to tie it all together. How to create a catchy title and a vision of the cover to show you what you want and/or need to include in your cookbook. How to begin a magnificent meal—your cookbook. Putting your personal taste into the pages. How to collect, test, and sort your recipes. How to get organized and get started. Prep time and cook time for your cookbook.

How to write your cookbook to feed all your potential markets. Think big—think food feast! Cookbook credentials. Deciding whether to self-publish or seek a commercial publisher. Pros and cons of both, and how to go about it. Beginning your budget. How to figure your cost and determine the size of your print run. Allocating funds for extras that sneak up and bite you. The price of promotion.

Chapter Three. Vegetables & Side Dishes 43

What do you want to serve on the side in your cookbook? What can you spice it up with to make it more enticing and a delicious read? Stories and anecdotes? Pithy sayings? Prep and cook times? Calorie counts? Nutritional analyses? Cooking hints and tips? Substitutions and serving suggestions? Presentations? Illustrations or clip art? What is going to give your cookbook its extra-special, taste-tempting appeal?

Chapter Four. Main Dishes 63

Now you're into the meat of the matter. Filling your cookbook with really good recipes that other cooks will prepare and enjoy. Writing your recipes. Flavoring your words to make them mouth-watering. Doing the details to make your recipes sound delicious. Consistency counts. How to serve your recipes with style. Finding the format and design for your cookbook that works for you. Page composition and layouts—presenting your recipes in an appealing manner; making them user-friendly. Typesetting; preparing camera-ready and press-ready copy.

Chapter Five. Breads & Rolls 77

Proofing your cookbook to make it perfect. Pricing your cookbook. Rising your cookbook to raise more sales. Selling advertising space. Printing promotional materials. Flyers, sell sheets, recipe cards, posters, refrigerator magnets, and postcards. Things to do while your cookbook is baking at the printer. The bread and butter of your cookbook. Doing pre-pub announcements and making advance sales to roll in the dough. Planning your promotions. Researching your markets. Writing enticing ads and press releases to sell the sizzle. How to make your cookbook stand out from the crowd.

Chapter Six. Desserts 87

Taste the sweet success of the fruits of your labors. Holding your cookbook in your hands is like having a delicious dessert. Launching your cookbook to the community and to the world. Having a huge kick-off party, a big hoopla to start the sales. Putting together a press kit. Doing the media blitz. Entering your cookbook in contests to win awards. Making premium sales. Doing direct mail. Listing your cookbook on websites and in catalogs. Showing off your cookbook. How to get rave reviews and obtain endorsements.

Chapter Seven. Cookies & Candy 93

How the cookie crumbles; how to make your cookbook available to everyone who wants to buy it. How to place your cookbook in bookstores and libraries. Little and local. Regional and national. Breaking into the major chains—Borders and Barnes & Noble. How to get the corporate book buyers to select your cookbook. Gift and gourmet shops. Doing the distribution route. Alternate avenues to pursue to get your cookbook into bookstores.

Chapter Eight. This & That 103

Super ways to make super sales. 101 ways to market and promote your cookbook. Getting on the gravy train to cover your sales beyond the bookstores. Sauces and seasonings not only spice up your food and make your meal delicious, they can make or break your cookbook.

Appendix A. Cookbook Printers 125

A comprehensive list of specialty cookbook printers, how to contact them, what they offer, and a price chart.

Appendix B. Cookbook Contests / Catalogs /
        Conferences 128

Cookbook contests you can enter your cookbook in. Catalogs to feature your cookbook in to give you wider coverage for your promotion dollars. Cookbook conferences you can attend to learn about writing and marketing your cookbook.

A list of websites for recipes and cooking information, culinary tie-in items, places to promote your cookbook on the Internet, and ways to market your cookbook through direct mail. Book fairs, trade and gift shows to show and sell your cookbook, and information about book exhibitors to showcase your cookbook.

A list of cookbook distributors and wholesalers, and a list of book reviewers.

A list of reference books about publishing and promoting, with a brief description of each book.

A list of Epicurean magazines to write for, with a brief description of each.

Foods & Flavors of San Antonio

Introduction

I wrote my first cookbook, *Really Good Recipes*, nine years ago because I love to cook and I'm a writer, and because I thought it would be fun to write a cookbook to share my recipes. Another reason I wrote it was because my daughters had moved away from home and kept calling me for my recipes.

The cookbook was a self-published compilation of my best original recipes; it also contained recipes I'd collected from friends over the years, recipes my mom had made, and recipes I'd found in magazines and modified to suit my tastes. It was a nice, kitchen-style cookbook served with homey touches that sold fairly well. I also gave away lots of copies to my friends and family.

Then I thought it would be fun to learn how to cook professionally, so I went back to school to study culinary arts. I didn't change careers from being a writer to becoming a chef, but I did learn how to cook a lot better. I also discovered some professional secrets that only chefs know, along with hundreds of delicious, restaurant-style recipes.

While in school, I wrote and self-published three more cookbooks—*Food Feasts*, *Best of the Barbecues*, and *The Cheapie Chicken Cookbook*—and learned a lot, through experience, about writing, marketing, promoting, and selling cookbooks on my own. When I finished school, I began writing *Cook Like a Chef*. My newest cookbook, *Foods & Flavors of San Antonio*, is in the process of being commercially published.

I learned a lot more in school than how to cook like a chef. I learned the ins and outs of writing and publishing cookbooks. It was self-taught, valuable knowledge that resulted in successful cookbooks. I'd like to share that knowledge with you by sharing my recipe for all the ingredients that go into making and marketing a cookbook.

This book is a guide that shows you how to create, cook, and serve your cookbook with style and flair. It offers food for thought by helping you become more knowledgeable about writing, publishing, and selling your cookbook; it provides plenty of know-how and generous portions of how-to for producing a cookbook. I hope it both invites and inspires you to write your cookbook.

Writing can be time-consuming and I don't want you to starve in the process of writing your cookbook, though I doubt that will happen as you're a good cook and you'll be testing lots of recipes to include in your cookbook. A few sample recipes are included in case you get hungry while reading this book or while working on your own cookbook. The recipes also show various page layouts, fillers, and text designs you can use in formatting your cookbook.

I'm sure you'll find the recipe for success in writing, publishing, and promoting your cookbook inside these pages.

Chapter One

Appetizers & Beverages

You may think that anyone can write a cookbook. You're right; they can. Anyone can put together a collection of recipes. But writing a good cookbook is a whole other story. And that's exactly what a good cookbook should be: a story. It should include more than great recipes that are well-written and easy to follow. It should have a theme, a focus, and a story line. It should offer delicious tidbits of information as well as serving a full course of taste and style on every page.

Beginning Your Cookbook

Before you begin, know why you want to write a cookbook. Do you want to share your recipes? Pass down recipes through your family to preserve traditions and heirloom recipes? Want to write a cookbook as a lark, because it would be fun? Perhaps you have a new twist on cooking that no one has done before? Do you want to create a cookbook to use as a fundraiser for your church, school, group, or charitable organization? Are you a professional in the culinary industry and want to teach? A chef with original recipes? Do you own a restaurant and want to attract more customers? Are you a caterer and want to enhance your business? Own a kitchen gourmet shop and want a profitable sideline to sell?

There are many reasons for writing a cookbook; all of them are good. What kind of cookbooks do you enjoy? What kind of cookbook do you want to write? Why do you want to write it? What do you want from publishing a cookbook? Go and find a pencil and more than a few pieces of paper. Sit down at the kitchen table with a cup of tea or coffee and list your reasons before you continue to read.

In addition to helping you become clear on why you want to write a cookbook, and for what purpose, your reasons will permeate and influence how you select your recipes and how you'll write and market your cookbook. Knowing the reasons you want to write a cookbook will show you how to develop your cookbook's personality and help you find and target potential markets.

Knowing your markets before you begin writing your cookbook will help you shape and define it, and will show you your niche in the marketplace where your cookbook will fit in nicely. It will help you determine how many copies to print, and will show you the way to all the possibilities of promoting your cookbook outside of bookstores and libraries.

As you're writing your cookbook, keep your buyer in mind. Who is going to buy your cookbook? Why will they buy it? What will they gain in return for purchasing your cookbook? What can you give them in your cookbook that is special and unique? What can you offer that is fresh and exciting, or has never been done before?

Write out a long list of potential buyers and the markets for your cookbook. Brainstorm a bit. Get your friends, family, co-workers, and the people in your group or organization to put their heads together and come up with ideas, even some outrageous and far-fetched ones. Stretch your imagination and include anyone who will be even remotely interested in buying your cookbook. Having this information and knowing who your buyers are at the beginning will be helpful in creating the concept for your cookbook and in positioning it in the marketplace.

It will also help you find non-bookstore outlets and premium sales when you're ready to promote and sell your cookbook. Look in Chapter Eight to gather some ideas, then cook up lots of your own to find creative outlets for your cookbook. You may even come up with a group or organization who will underwrite the cost of producing and promoting your cookbook.

Gathering Ideas as well as Recipes

You'll be creating and cooking your cookbook from scratch. Think about how you want to style your cookbook. What do you want it to say? What story do you want to tell? What kind of a feel do you want your cookbook to have? Put your personal taste into the pages. Come up with a cookbook concept that has a distinct theme and focus. Make the story line and fillers in your cookbook appealing and appetizing.

Take another break from reading and create the outline for your cookbook, a road map that will guide you during the construction of your cookbook and lead you on the path to publication. Write down your thoughts and feelings about the cookbook you want to write. Clearly and thoroughly define the scope, theme, and focus of your cookbook. How do you want to shape it? What do you want to feed your readers? What kind of recipes do you want to include?

Tie it all together with your story line. A cookbook isn't just a cookbook. It's much more. It's an armchair culinary trip. Many cooks read cookbooks like a novel or an interesting nonfiction book. Tell a story in your cookbook and include fillers. Weave a common theme and thread throughout your recipes.

Here are a few examples to help you get started: My first cookbook, *Really Good Recipes*, was about sharing food with friends and family. I wanted to share my recipes and some anecdotes about cooking for my daughters. The theme and tone of my cookbook was that nurturing through the nourishment of food is what makes a kitchen the heart of a home.

Several cookbooks later, after a two-year stint at a culinary arts college, I wrote *Cook Like a Chef*. The story line was exactly what the title implied. I wanted to teach home cooks how to cook like a chef by sharing cooking secrets and shortcuts I'd learned, as well as providing great recipes I'd developed. I included an anecdote— called a headnote—with almost every recipe. Chef's tips were sprinkled throughout the cookbook. I featured professional presentations for serving. Not too many cookbooks do this and that's one of the things which made this cookbook special, what made it stand out from the crowd.

My most recent cookbook, *Foods & Flavors of San Antonio*, has great Tex-Mex recipes from local restaurants and residents, plus a tour of the sights and attractions, along with a calendar of food festivals and fiestas. I wrote this cookbook when I moved to San Antonio and began exploring the city and what it had to offer.

The *Los Barrios Family Cookbook* by Diana Barrios Treviño is a two-in-one kind of cookbook. The anecdotes are about family and are centered around memories of food; the recipes are ones that are prepared and served in their restaurant.

You can make your cookbook as unique and individual as you are. Mollie Katzen has written several vegetarian cookbooks which feature hand-lettered recipes and her whimsical artwork. One of her cookbooks—*The Enchanted Broccoli Forest*—offers a catchy title and is also one of the recipes.

Cooking with Class was published by a college preparatory school as a fundraiser. The dividers were relative to attending college. Admissions was for Appetizers; Electives was for Vegetables. Food facts and helpful hints were included with many recipes, teaching readers the fine art of food preparation.

Fix-It and Forget-It Cookbook by Dawn Ranck and Phyllis Good focuses entirely on cooking—feasting as they say—with your slow cooker. Recipes are from crock pot cooks all over the country. This cookbook is enormously popular; it's a New York Times bestseller. It has inspired several spin-off cookbooks: *Fix-It and Forget-It Lightly* and *Fix-It and Forget-It Recipes for Entertaining*.

There are many health-related cookbooks on the market and they sell very well. *Weight Watchers New 365 Day Menu Cookbook* offers complete meals for every day of the year, along with a nutritional analysis for each recipe. (By the way, there's a great recipe for zucchini meatloaf on page 25 of that cookbook.) The low-carb craze, inspired by *The South Beach Diet*, continues with plenty of cookbooks serving delicious, creative, low-carb recipes. If you're doing a health cookbook, be sure you have the credentials to back it up.

Where Hearts Gather by Susan Cannon offers recipes and remembrances as a tribute to her mother-in-law.

Top Secret Restaurant Recipes by Todd Wilbur shares the not-so-secret-anymore recipes prepared in popular restaurants, along with illustrations and step-by-step directions for replicating the recipes.

Tastes of Texas was written as a fundraiser for firefighters; it includes recipes from firefighters all over the state of Texas.

There are many different themes for a cookbook; each one tells a story. Some cookbooks blend two or more categories together. Try some of these themes on for size:

Generic. Includes recipes and headnotes, but little else.

Family. Treasured, time-tested family recipes, remembrances, and stories, all caught in a collection, are family-oriented cookbooks.

Restaurant. Recipes are those that are prepared in the restaurant, along with a slice of history about the restaurant and/or the chef.

Diet. Cookbooks which feature healthy recipes for low-carb, low-fat, heart-healthy, or for diabetics, are a few of the many types of health-related cookbooks.

Regional. Covers a specific region or type of cooking, such as Tex-Mex, Cajun, or Midwest cooking. The story line is specific to the area and type of food.

Ethnic. Cookbooks about Thai or Chinese cuisine, to name a few, featuring recipes from a specific culture, are ethnic cookbooks.

Historical. Recipes from a time gone by, interspersed with stories about cooking during that era, or cookbooks that share the local lore and history along with current recipes.

One Topic. Cookbooks that cover only cookies, seafood, or soups, are centered on one topic.

Food Specific. Cookbooks that cover one food and the myriad ways to cook and serve it are food specific. For example, Hormel has written *Spam: The Cookbook*.

Cooking Specific. Cookbooks solely about crock pot cooking, microwaving, or grilling, are cooking specific.

Appliance Specific. Cookbooks on woks, bamboo steamers, or bread machines, feature recipes to make using those appliances.

Cookbooks can combine one or more of the above themes. For example, a bed and breakfast cookbook might include recipes served for brunch, as well as the regional flair and history of the establishment. It may also include travel tips and local information. Interesting anecdotes are the icing on the cake.

Begin your cookbook by cooking up lots of creative ideas for it. Once you know your theme and story, the kind of recipes and other material you want to share, and you have your outline in place, you can start collecting, testing, sorting, and writing the recipes that will fit into your cookbook.

Creating a Cover

It may seem a bit premature to work on the cover of your cookbook before you start putting your recipes together, but doing the cover first can help you shape your cookbook and give you even more ideas of what you want to include. It will show you your cookbook's personality.

Most of the cookbook printers listed in Appendix A offer an array of colorful cookbook covers to choose from or you can create a custom cover for your cookbook that is original and unique. Choose from one of theirs or create your own cover that will fit the theme and focus of your cookbook, a cover that will convey what's inside.

Along with your cover concept, come up with a title. Your title says it all. While the title you choose now may or may not change as you write your cookbook, it will provide a foundation and a steppingstone as you sum up the cookbook you want to write in the words of your title.

While you're cooking up ideas for your cookbook cover and simmering ideas for the title through your mind, look through cookbooks in bookstores and the ones you have at home. Look at their covers and read the titles. What does the cover convey? What does the title imply? Does it offer a benefit or a promise? A sneak peek into what you'll find inside the pages? Are you getting hungry just looking at the cover and reading the title? Or does the cover and title leave you feeling a little empty?

Having a great cover and a catchy, come-hither title will do more for your cookbook than you can imagine. Besides covering your cookbook in style and showing/telling readers—potential buyers—right up front what your cookbook is all about, a great cover and a catchy title can make or break your cookbook, no matter what's inside.

You've heard the adage, "You can't judge a book by looking at its cover." While that may be true for people and situations, and a few booklovers, a plain, blah, bland, or downright bad cover won't get your cookbook anywhere but a few copies that you'll give to friends.

Your cover and title will have to stand up to plenty of people in the book industry—distributors, sales reps, corporate book buyers, and bookstore owners, to name a few—who will decide to carry your cookbook based on the cover and title alone. They will barely give your cookbook a cursory glance—two to three seconds at most—before they decide to carry it or refuse it. To them, books—especially cookbooks—are a dime a dozen.

Your cookbook won't fare any better in the bookstore if you have a mediocre cover and a title that says next to nothing. People browsing in a bookstore are more generous with their time. They will spend eight to ten seconds looking at your cover and reading your title before they decide to either read on or put your cookbook back on the shelf.

Since most books are shelved spine out in libraries and book-stores, your title needs to immediately capture the attention of the person reading it so they will pull it off the shelf. If the title doesn't draw them, or interest them in wanting more, your cookbook won't even be looked at; it will be passed over in favor of another catchy title that's more appealing.

Create a terrific title and a vision of what you want the cover to look like. This will help show you what you want and/or need to include in your cookbook. Your cover, and the concept it conveys, will coordinate with the type of cookbook you want to write and with your story line.

Creating the theme and focus, coming up with the cover concept and title, and finding your story line, will set the tone for your cookbook. Somewhere in the middle of all your creativity in imagining your cookbook to be all that it can be and more, do one more, very important, thing.

Come up with a selling handle for your cookbook. A selling handle is a bite of information that completely describes your cookbook in as few words as possible. Your selling handle is longer than your title and shorter than a paragraph. Think in terms of a subtitle. Your selling handle can be your subtitle.

The purpose of a subtitle is to clearly and concisely define and describe what the book is all about. If the title doesn't supply it, a subtitle implies a benefit and/or a promise. Be sure your cookbook lives up to its title, and subtitle, if you have one. It goes without saying that you'll provide the benefit and deliver on your promise inside the pages.

Look again at the cookbooks in your kitchen. How would you describe them in twenty-five words or less? A mouthful of information is what you want to provide in your selling handle. For example—and this is a bad example to show you what not to say—your selling handle could be: A collection of recipes to make your mouth water and tempt your taste buds. This doesn't give you a clear idea of what's really inside. All you can surmise from this is that there are recipes inside the cookbook.

Here are some much better examples, taken from commercially published cookbooks: *Healthy Homestyle Cooking: 200 of Your Favorite Family Recipes—With a Fraction of the Fat.* This tells you exactly what's inside. *Classic Tex-Mex and Texas Cooking: Authentic Recipes with Big, Bold Flavors.* Texas is known for being big and bold. The cookbook promises authentic, spicy recipes.

Here's one you probably won't want to bite at: *1,001 Low-Carb Recipes: Hundreds of delicious recipes to make low-carb maintenance easy and fun.* This subtitle makes a glaring mistake that is misleading. The title says 1,001 yet the subtitle says hundreds. It would read better if the 'hundreds of' was dropped and the subtitle started with 'delicious.' It would also be better to put the subtitle in initial caps, not in lower case. Here's another one with a bad bite: *Rachael Ray 30-Minute GET REAL Meals.* While her show on the food network is great, the title doesn't say what the cookbook is really about. You gather that the meals take thirty minutes to prepare but there is nothing which tells you the cookbook is about low-carb cooking.

Here are some good bites: *Fix-It and Forget-It Cookbook: Feasting with your Slow Cooker. Betty Crocker's One-Dish Meals: Casse-*

roles, Skillet Meals, Stir-Fries and More for Easy, Everyday Din-ners. Think-Thin One-Pot Meals: Over 100 Delicious and Satisfying Recipes Good for You and Your Body. The South Beach Diet: The Delicious, Doctor-Designed, Foolproof Plan for Fast and Healthy Weight Loss.

Get the idea? All these bites are on the front cover. They either offer a benefit or imply a promise; some do both. Most of all, they tell you what's inside. Grab your pencil and paper again. Create your selling handle, your mouthful of information, your bite. You want people to bite at buying your cookbook, so give them a bite that's completely appealing, delicious, and descriptive.

You may think that a sentence or two about your cookbook is easy to write but you may be wrong. Give your selling handle careful thought and consideration. After you write your bite, hone it, cut it, rewrite it, shape it, sculpt it, tear it up, and start all over again until you come up with the perfect description of your cookbook.

You'll use your selling handle many times: in your promotional materials, in press releases, in talking about your cookbook to poten-tial buyers, and in persuading book people to take a liking to your cookbook. Sales reps will use your handle to sell your cookbook to libraries, bookstores, and other retail markets. We'll get into all of this later in the book, but for now, write your bite.

When you've done this, create a mock cover. Either use one of the cookbook printer's covers or draw a sketch of what you want your cover to look like. Color it in and letter in the title. Make a color photocopy of it and put it on the wall above your computer or the desk where you'll be writing your cookbook. This will help inspire you on to creating a wonderful cookbook because you can envision the finished project.

Collecting Recipes

Now that you have your kitchen table notes, and your framed cover, begin to collect, test, and write your recipes, along with the story line and theme to fit the cookbook you have in mind.

If you're using your own recipes for a personal or a family cook-book, you already have your collection. If you're gathering recipes from co-workers, members in your group, school, church, or organization, let everyone know by sending out a call for recipes. There are several ways to do this. Post a notice on the bulletin board, have a cookbook meeting, send out a memo or a letter, or call everyone you'd like to get recipes from and ask them to contribute. Have everyone follow the same format in writing their recipes. If you're doing a community cookbook and want to gather local recipes, send out a press release or place an ad in the local newspaper.

Taste-Testing Recipes

If you're using your own recipes, you've already tested them, probably many times. If you're using recipes from other people or ones you've found in magazines or other cookbooks, prepare them several times to be sure the recipe directions are clear, do-able, and that they taste delicious. Tweak them a bit, make changes and vary the seasonings to make the recipes unique. Include ingredients that weren't originally in the recipe. Rewrite the methodology, which is the directions for making the recipe.

By the way, the list of ingredients in recipes can't be copyrighted, so you're free to use any recipe you want. However, it's not a good idea to copy someone else's cookbook and claim it as your own. Re-do recipes from other cookbooks to make them uniquely yours. If you are going to borrow a recipe verbatim from a cookbook, write to the publisher and request permission. Be sure to acknowledge the author and cookbook title in your copied recipe.

If other people are going to prepare and taste-test the recipes you'll be including in your cookbook, here are some tips for recipe testers from *Making Sure Your Recipes Measure Up*, by the International Association of Culinary Professionals.

• Write your name and the date of your test on each recipe you test.
• Test when you are not rushed or feeling harried.
• Test the recipe exactly as written.
• Read through the entire recipe and shop for all the ingredients in advance so you have them on hand.

• Assemble and measure out all the recipe ingredients before beginning to prepare it.

• Use graduated measuring cups for dry ingredients. To measure 1 cup granulated sugar, for example, overfill the cup, then scrape across the top to level, using a knife or a long spatula.

• Use the dip and sweep method to measure flour. Dip the measure into the flour so the measure is overfilled, then scrape across the top to level, using a knife or a long spatula.

• Use the size and type of cooking container or baking dish that is called for. A different size or material might change the cooking time, or even the texture of a dish.

• Check off each ingredient as it is added to a recipe.

• Use a timer, and set it to the minimum baking / cooking / beating time indicated in the recipe. Note if your times or results come out different from what was specified, and write down your results in the recipe margins.

• If you notice mistakes, such as typographical errors or ingredients left out of the text, correct them on the recipe.

• If any instructions seem confusing, too hard, or overly time consuming, mention the problems you encountered in the margins or at the end of the recipe.

• Look for anything that is different from what the recipe indicates, such as: Wrong consistency / harder or easier to work with than expected; wrong baking / cooking time; wrong yield (or no yield); wrong pan size (or no size); a direction that doesn't make sense; and anything that doesn't work as the recipe said it would.

• Look for obvious mistakes, such as ingredients that are not in the right order or are dropped, oven turned on too soon or too late, and stove temperature too high or too low.

• Look for anything that might seem confusing to a cook who isn't familiar with this recipe or this procedure. Also, offer any suggestions for improving, streamlining, or simplifying the recipe.

• Fill out the recipe rating sheet while the results are still fresh in your mind. If you've shared the food with someone, also include their reaction to the taste-testing.

Rating Sheet

Date of Test _____

Recipe Name _____

Tester's Name _____

Rate the recipe from 1 – 10, 10 being the best.

Taste _____ Texture _____
Appearance _____ Overall Appeal _____

Elaborate on your scoring.

_____

_____

_____

How did this recipe compare with similar ones you have tried?

_____

_____

_____

Was this recipe worth the effort?

Yes _____ Not sure _____ No _____

Elaborate on your answer.

_____

_____

_____

A few fun ways to test recipes, if you are working with a group, is to have a pot luck dinner with everyone preparing different recipes. You can get great feedback this way, not to mention a great meal. If you're doing a cookbook by yourself, enlist the help of your friends and family. Have everyone cook different recipes, then get together for a feast.

Another interesting way to test recipes is to have a friend make the same recipe you are testing. Invite your friend over for dinner and taste both recipes at the same time on the same plate. You might be surprised that one recipe, prepared by two people, can taste amazingly different. Compare notes on how you each prepared the recipe.

Reviewing and Sorting Recipes

When you've collected and tested all your recipes, and decided which ones you want to include in your cookbook, sort them into related groups in the food chain. Most cookbooks follow a natural order of progression from appetizers through desserts, just as if you were eating a meal.

Do a preliminary edit to shape the recipes into the format you plan to follow. A few things to look for include: making sure the abbreviations are consistent, the recipes are written in the style you've chosen, they're clear and easy to follow, and they fit in with the theme of your cookbook. You'll be doing a final edit later. For now, begin to shape your recipes.

Prep Time and Cook Time

How long will it take you to prepare and complete your cookbook? This depends on several variables. First determine what you want your cookbook to say. Find its voice and personality.

From your kitchen table notes, look over the outline of how you're planning to structure your cookbook, what you want to include in each section, and what your story line is. Your outline will probably take several weeks to a month or two to come together completely. Your outline forms the foundation for your cookbook and will get you off to a running start. Your outline also helps you pull your cookbook together into a cohesive whole.

Once you have that in place, begin to collect and test recipes. This process can take anywhere from several weeks to several months, depending on the number of recipes you're putting into your cookbook, if you're working by yourself or with a cookbook committee, and how much testing needs to be done.

While you're collecting recipes, or even before you begin, decide whether you want to self-publish your cookbook or have it published by a commercial publisher. This will influence how you proceed in various parts of writing your cookbook.

If you decide to self-publish, you'll need to credential your cookbook. Sending for the forms, filling them in, returning them, and waiting for your materials may take several months. Plan accordingly. Get this into motion early in writing your cookbook so you don't slow down your progress by having to wait for important items before you go to press. (See Chapter Two.)

Here's how your timeline might go:

1. Decide to write a cookbook.

2. Develop theme, focus, and story line. Write a detailed outline. Create a cover concept, come up with a title and a selling handle. One week to one month.

3. Collect, test, and sort recipes. Two to six months.

4. Write your recipes and finalize your cookbook. Three to six months, maybe as long as a year.

5. If you are self-publishing, you can expect to have your cookbook in hand after a thirty to forty-five day turnaround time from the printer. If you have a commercial publisher, your cookbook will be printed anywhere from six months to two years after you finish writing it and the publisher has finished editing it.

During the process of writing your cookbook, determine how you will promote, market, and sell your cookbook. Write down ideas as they come to you to expand on the marketing list you wrote earlier. Create a workable budget that will cover all your expenses and give you a nice profit. You'll need to do this even if a commercial publisher has accepted your cookbook.

Set a reasonable and realistic timetable for each part of the process. You know how much you can accomplish, you know how you work, and how much time you have available to write your cookbook. You don't have to rigidly stick to the timetable presented here. It's a guideline to keep you moving in the right direction—toward publication.

Chapter Two

Soups & Salads

Write your cookbook to feed all the hungry people who will buy it. Your buyers are your potential markets. Think big. Think food feast! Not only for your readers in giving them a great cookbook filled with wonderful recipes, but for giving yourself a nice profit, along with a wonderful sense of satisfaction. You want to enjoy the fruits of your labors. Write the kind of cookbook you would buy for yourself.

Commercial Publishing

If you decide to go the commercial route—finding a publisher to publish your cookbook—be aware that this is a tough market to crack but it's not impossible. You'll need impressive credentials. This doesn't mean you have to be a chef. It means you can parlay your experience and expertise into presenting yourself as a professional.

To find a commercial publisher, go to the library and look through several reference books which contain a comprehensive listing of book publishers and their interests. This will help you research potential publishers who would be the best ones for your cookbook. Look through *Writer's Market*, published by Writer's Digest Books, *The Writer's Handbook*, published by The Writer Books, and *Jeff Herman's Guide to Book Publishers, Editors, & Literary Agents*, published by Three Dog Press.

Read through the listings to determine if they publish cookbooks. Many of them do but there's a catch. Some only publish regional or health-specific cookbooks. Some listings state this but other listings simply say cookbooks. When you've found publishers that you think are right for your cookbook, visit their website and look through their titles. Take your research a few steps further. Visit bookstores to see the quality of the cookbooks they publish, and to see if their cookbooks are actually on the shelves.

While you're in the library, you may also want to look through *Writer's Market Guide to Literary Agents*, published by Writer's Digest Books, if you want to find an agent to represent your cookbook. Sometimes these books can be checked out but since they're reference books, your library may only have one copy that has to stay in the library. If you'd prefer to buy the books, they are available in bookstores for about $30.00 each.

When you've completed your market research and found several publishers and/or agents you'd like to approach, write a proposal. Your cookbook proposal will give the editor at the publishing house, or the agent, important information about your cookbook that will help them decide if they want to publish it, or represent it, in the case of an agent.

Writing a Cookbook Proposal

A cookbook proposal follows a certain format and includes information that is necessary for the editor or agent to know. Your cookbook doesn't have to be finished before you propose on it. When you've got your outline and ideas firmly in place, and you're about one-third of the way through writing it, is a good time to start shopping it around.

Appendix G shows a query letter and sample cookbook proposal. Personalize your cookbook proposal to fit your cookbook. Mention its unique attributes and features, what makes it special—and most importantly—what your marketing and promotion plans are, what will make your cookbook sell, who it will appeal to, and why they will buy it.

Your proposal begins with your query letter, followed by a Title Page, Proposal Contents, Overview, Author Bio, Table of Contents with Chapter Summaries, Competition, Promotion and Marketing, Book Specs, Sample Recipes, and a SASE. Paginate it continuously, beginning with the Overview, with a running head that shows your cookbook title, your last name, and the page number. Broken down into bite-size pieces, here's how your proposal will present both you and your cookbook:

Query Letter. This introduces you and your cookbook. It's a one-page snapshot of what your cookbook is about, who you are, and what you've done relative to writing your cookbook. The first paragraph is about your cookbook. The second paragraph is about you and your writing credits and cooking credentials. The third paragraph maps your major potential markets; it tells who the cookbook will appeal to and why they will buy it. The last paragraph closes the letter and shows the enclosures.

The query letter introduces your cookbook to the potential publisher. Make it short, sweet, and to the point. Include only the important information the editor needs to know to pique her interest and lure her into reading the rest of your proposal. Include facts and figures. Editors think in concrete terms of book sales, so show her you've researched the market and how large it is.

Think of your query letter as an appetizer. You want to whet the editor's or agent's appetite so he or she will read the remainder of your proposal to see if your cookbook would be right for them. Don't stuff it with too much information; you'll be presenting the other important ingredients in the remaining portions of your proposal.

Title Page. This is exactly what it sounds like. It covers your proposal pages. Show your cookbook title, subtitle if you have one, selling handle, and your name, address, phone number(s), email, and website. Include the number of recipes and the page count for your cookbook or an approximate page count if your cookbook is still in the works.

Proposal Contents. This lists the parts of your proposal and gives page numbers. It enables the editor or agent to go to the different parts of your proposal easily. Most agents and editors flip through and scan a book proposal to begin with, much the same way you do when you're looking through a cookbook in the bookstore and deciding whether to buy it or put it back on the shelf.

Overview. This is a one-page description of what your cookbook is about, how you will prepare it, cook it, and serve it. Expand on the first paragraph of your query letter. Be a bit more conversational.

Show the benefits that cooks will receive by reading your cookbook and using your recipes, aside from delicious meals. List special features that your cookbook offers. Think in terms of a back cover blurb.

Author Bio or About the Author. Write this in the third person, as if you were writing about someone else. This makes it easier to write a glowing account of yourself. Who are you and what have you done that qualifies you to write your cookbook? Present yourself as a professional. Even if you only klutz around the kitchen on weekends, cooking and creating delicious recipes, make your bio sound as if you're the chef of the century. Be creative (and truthful).

If you've been cooking for thirty years, say so. If you teach cooking classes at the community college, write that down. If you've appeared on television to talk about food, have done cooking demonstrations, been interviewed in the paper, won cooking contests or awards, have a degree in culinary arts, or given lectures related to food, be sure to mention it.

If you've self-published a cookbook or been commercially published, even if it wasn't a cookbook, or had recipes published in the local newspaper or in food magazines, that makes you a published author. List your publishing credits. If you haven't yet been published, don't say so. It's obvious you want to get your cookbook published. Put all your accomplishments in a positive light.

Anything and everything you've done relating to cooking and food helps to qualify you as an expert. Did you win the chili cook-off at last year's 4th of July festivities? Are you a server in a restaurant and occasionally help out in the kitchen? Do you belong to the IACP—International Association of Culinary Professionals—or another professional culinary organization? Are you glued to the Food Network on TV? Do you collect cookbooks? Do you make the best potluck dinner at church or for community events? You get the picture. Write a recipe of yourself as the accomplished cook that you are.

If your cooking credentials are a bit weak, team up with a chef to co-author your cookbook. This may help you get your first cookbook commercially published because publishers will take you and your cookbook more seriously. Chefs have plenty of culinary connections and sales avenues to help promote and market the cookbook.

Many chefs would be delighted to co-author or collaborate on a cookbook because they usually don't have time to write one. They'd supply some or most of the recipes, lend their name and culinary expertise to your cookbook, and wind up also being a published cookbook author, which looks good on their resume and gives them more prestige. It would be a good partnership for both of you. Once you're commercially published, it's easier to get a second cookbook published on your own.

Table of Contents with Chapter Summaries. This shows the courses your cookbook will serve. This is where your outline will come in handy. Give a few of the recipe titles in each chapter, along with a brief description that includes the story line you'll weave through the cookbook. State the number of recipes in each chapter.

Competition. Compare your cookbook to four or five cookbooks which are similar to yours. These are the ones your cookbook will be competing with on the bookstore shelves. Show how your cookbook stacks up and what it offers that comparable cookbooks don't. Show how your cookbook is different from or better than similar cookbooks on the market. Tell what makes your cookbook special and unique. Your publisher will need to know this information to determine what features make your cookbook stand out, and also helps them know how to position your cookbook in the marketplace.

Promotion and Marketing. Since there are so many cookbooks out there, your publisher will need—and require—your help to make your cookbook a success, to sell lots of copies. What can you do to help promote and sell your cookbook? Can you sell it through your cooking classes? Do you rent a booth at food festivals and book fairs? Do you attend culinary trade events? Do you have a website or food blog you can showcase it on? Are you willing to speak to groups about your cookbook? Can you do cooking demonstrations and book signings? Do you know a famous chef who might be willing to endorse your cookbook or write a foreword?

The promotion and marketing section is perhaps the most important part of your proposal. You have to show that you are ready, willing, and able to sell lots of copies, that there are many lucrative markets for your cookbook, and you know how to reach them. Give this section a lot of thought. Brainstorm on the numerous ways you can help sell mega copies of your cookbook. This can be the deciding factor in whether a publisher will take your cookbook.

Commercial publishers want an author with a platform. A platform is a cookbook author who has media experience and can provide or knows how to tap into lucrative markets to sell the cookbook, such as cooking classes, a TV show or appearances on national television, lectures, good culinary connections, a targeted mailing list, and things of this nature.

Do everything you can from submitting recipes to newspapers and magazines, writing articles or blogs about food, doing cooking demonstrations on TV, and anything else you can think of relating to food and cooking, to show your publisher that you have a platform to stand on that will catapult your cookbook into serving a huge market.

Book Specs. Show the specifications for your cookbook and where you are in terms of completion. State the number of recipes you plan to include and the page count, even though you've put this information on the title page. State if you have charts, tables, illustrations, clip art, menus, resource guides, a glossary, or other items. It's understood that you will have an index but mention it here.

Let the publisher know how long it will take to complete your cookbook by giving a delivery date. It always takes longer than you think it will to finish writing your cookbook, so give yourself a time cushion. Most publishers want your cookbook six months after they make an offer for it. Note whether you can provide a computer disk when you send in the hard copy of your cookbook and if you have a Mac or a PC. Most publishers require both a disk and a hard copy, which is the physical pages of your manuscript.

You may also want to mention your vision for your cookbook. How would you like to see it published? A trade size softcover, perfect bound, an 8-1/2 x 11 hardcover with color photographs, or some other format? If you have ideas and suggestions about what you'd like the cover to look like, include that information here.

Sample Recipes. Include at least one recipe from each chapter. Show off your best recipes. Make them so mouth-wateringly delicious that the editor or agent will rush right into the kitchen to prepare them. In addition to your sample recipes, you might like to include a list of recipes you plan to include in your cookbook.

SASE. A self-addressed, stamped envelope (#10 business size) is required to receive a reply from the editor or agent. Even though you've included your address, phone number, and email on both your query letter and the title page of your proposal, it's common courtesy and a publishing protocol to send a SASE.

Self-Publishing

If you decide to self-publish, you'll be doing much, much more than writing a cookbook. You'll be doing everything yourself or in combination with others in your group or organization, perhaps on a cookbook committee. If you have an entrepreneurial spirit, like to be in control of and in charge of everything, and are a do-it-yourselfer, this is probably the path you'll want to take. Self-publishing works especially well for groups and organizations who publish a fundraising cookbook, as well as for families who put together a cookbook of favorite family recipes. Individuals who write a cookbook may have to work harder at it since they are doing it solo.

By self-publishing, you're creating a business; you need to be businesslike about it. If you're an individual, it's a good idea to have a publisher name. This looks more professional and will actually help to sell more copies of your cookbook. If you're creating a fundraising cookbook with your group, you'll probably be using the organization's name. Choose a publisher name that sounds professional, one that easily and clearly identifies your publishing company as a publishing company, not a cottage industry. For example, I chose Cozy Kitchens as my publisher name. It was fine for the first cookbook, but didn't wear well when I began self-publishing more professional cookbooks.

If you plan to publish more than one cookbook and grow your cookbook publishing company, choose a name that will grow with you. A few words of advice: Do not use your name as part of your publisher name, such as Conner Cookbooks. This marks you as an amateur. Don't use the word cookbook as part of your publisher name. People—both consumers and those in the publishing industry, such as bookstores and distributors—will know you're a self-publisher and may not take your cookbook seriously.

To use a publisher name, you'll need to apply for an Assumed Name Certificate with your city or county, and run a legal notice for three weeks before you receive the affidavit of publication and can begin using your publisher name. An Assumed Name Certificate is a legal document which states you are doing business as (dba) the name of the publishing company.

If you're working on a committee putting together a fundraising or a community cookbook, and you'll only be selling it to people in your organization and locally, you may or may not need to incorporate as a business depending on your circumstances. Check with an attorney to follow the proper procedure.

If you're an individual, self-publishing your cookbook, this makes you self-employed and the sole proprietor of your business. You'll need to keep detailed records and receipts of your income and expenses because you'll be filing Schedule C (Profit or Loss From Business) and Schedule SE (Self-Employment Tax) which will be attached to your federal 1040 income tax return. Even if you're commercially published, you'll need to keep accurate records of your business income and expenses, and file both Schedule C and SE on your tax return.

If you'll be selling your cookbook to the general public, you'll have to charge sales tax. Apply for a retail business tax number from your state capitol. They will tell you how much sales tax to charge, and will periodically—quarterly or semi-annually—send you forms to report the tax on and to pay any taxes due.

Being a business allows you to claim business deductions. Some of these deductions include the cost of printing* (all, some, or none of it), promotional materials, postage, phone calls, pens, pencils, paper, start-up costs (ISBN log, database fees for distributors, setting up your website, etc.), ink cartridges for your printer, stationery (envelopes, labels, and letterhead), and miscellaneous items.

*The IRS changes their requirements on this every few years. In any given tax year, they'll allow you to deduct the cost of your print run as a business expense. Their usual posture is that you can't deduct the cost of printing up front. Your printing bill will be the cost of goods sold (COGS). This is the unit price for each cookbook.

Your cookbooks are considered inventory. When you receive money for cookbooks sold, it won't be considered income until the monies accumulate to cover the cost of your inventory. You won't have to pay federal and state taxes on monies received until your COGS earn out and you show a profit after all your other business deductions. After your COGS earn out, you'll begin to make a profit, unless your other business expenses eat it up.

Business expenses also include items like the cost of this book (reference material), cooking and writing classes (education/training) you attend to enhance the material in your cookbook or to learn a new technique, promotional materials, and home office expenses. The IRS is very picky about home office expenses.

You can take a standard mileage deduction for your trips to the post office, bookstore, library, events you attend to promote your cookbook, and anywhere else you go in connection with writing, publishing, and promoting your cookbook. In some cases, you may be able to deduct a portion of your car payments, cost of gas, maintenance and repairs, insurance, tolls, and parking fees instead of the standard mileage deduction.

You may be able to amortize—spread out over the course of several years—your start-up costs. You may be able to claim a section 179 depreciation on your computer, printer, office furniture, and other major business purchases if they are bought in the year you start up your business or you may be able to take a percentage of their cost if they are put into service in your start-up year.

All your investment in your cookbook publishing company is considered at risk. Your business will have to show a profit within three years or in two out of five years. If not, the IRS will consider your venture a hobby, not a business, and will disallow all your deductions while making you pay taxes on your income.

IRS requirements stipulate that a publisher be on an accrual basis, rather than a cost basis. This means your cash flow is not what it appears to be. You count income when you earn it, not when you receive it. This can all be a bit confusing, so it might be wise to consult an accountant.

Because publishing your cookbook makes you a business, you may want to have a business checking account in your publisher name. You'll have to provide the bank with a copy of your Assumed Name Certificate. You may also want to obtain a toll-free number, and VISA and MasterCard merchant accounts to make it easier for your customers to buy your cookbook.

You may want to have a business address. Some self-publishers obtain a post office box. Not a good idea; this makes you look like an amateur and ranks you as a beginner. You want to present a professional image. A street address will give your publishing company and your cookbook prestige.

If you're creating a cookbook in conjunction with your group, you can use the organization's street address. If you're an individual, you can use your home address (also not a good idea) or you can rent a business address. Look in the phone book under Office Space. Some leasing companies provide corporate business support services, such as telephone answering, secretarial services, meeting rooms, and fax service, as well as a business mailing address, without you having to rent actual office space.

Credentialing Your Cookbook

If you self-publish, you'll want your cookbook to be as professional as possible if you plan to sell it outside of a small circle. You'll need an ISBN—International Standard Book Number—which will enable bookstores to carry and sell your cookbook. An ISBN is like a social security number for a book. It uniquely identifies your cookbook with a publisher prefix and an individual numerical sequence. Obtain an ISBN log from the International Standard Book Numbering Agency, R. R. Bowker, 630 Central Avenue, New Providence, NJ 07974. Phone: 877/310-7333. Website: www.isbn.org. The fee for an ISBN log is $275.00 for a block of 10 numbers. Get your ISBN log right away. Many other things in the publishing process hinge on having this.

You'll need to obtain a bar code embedded with your ISBN and price, and perhaps also a UPC code, so that bookstores and other retail outlets, such as grocery stores, can scan and sell your cookbook. Your printer can do this for you at a minimal charge.

If you want libraries to buy your cookbook, it's a good idea to have a Library of Congress Catalog Card Number. Self-published books are not eligible for Cataloging-in-Publication Data (CIP), which allows libraries to easily catalog and purchase books for their patrons. In lieu of CIP and to make your cookbook attractive to the library market, request a Preassigned Library of Congress Catalog Card Number (LCCN) from the Library of Congress, Cataloging-in-Publication Division, 101 Independence Avenue, S.E., Washington, DC 20540-4320. Phone: 202/707-6346. http://pcn.loc.gov/pcn. Complete your application online or send for this no later than two months prior to going to press; the earlier the better. You'll show this number, along with your ISBN, on the verso (copyright) page of your cookbook. After your cookbook is published, you'll send them a complimentary copy for reference-checking purposes.

You'll want to let bookstores and libraries know your cookbook is coming out and provide them with the information they need to order from you. Do your advance book information (ABI) after you receive your ISBN log. Bowker will email you a user ID and password that allows you to input your new book information on their website—www.bowkerlink.com—six months before your cookbook is published. This puts your cookbook information in the databases of *Books in Print* and *Forthcoming Books*, which all bookstores and libraries subscribe to.

Although recipes can't be copyrighted, you can copyright the remaining information in your cookbook, such as headnotes, text for your story line, commentary, anecdotes, cooking methodology, artwork, and things of that nature. Obtain Form TX from the Library of Congress, Copyright Office, 101 Independence Avenue, S.E., Washington, DC 20559-6000. Phone: 202/707-3000. www.copyright.gov. The fee is $45.00 plus a copy of your published cookbook.

Another way to copyright your cookbook is to put the copyright symbol ©, the year of publication, and your name on the verso page of your cookbook. This is standard practice. Copyright law states that once you commit words to paper, those words are copyrighted as your original work for your lifetime plus 70 years. Additionally, place the phrase All Rights Reserved on the verso page.

Cooking Up Your Credentials

Make yourself look like a professional. If you plan to seek a commercial publisher, you will need cooking credentials. If you plan to self-publish, your cooking credentials will serve to make you and your cookbook credible. You've probably already gathered a lot of ideas about how to do this in the Author Bio, and by thinking about your culinary adventures and accomplishments.

Begin, if you haven't already, submitting recipes to food magazines and to the food editor at the local newspaper to get your recipes published. (See Appendix F for a list of food magazines.) If you decide to pursue commercial publication, you can show your publishing credits because you've had your recipes published.

If you go the self-publishing route, you can put a brief bio on the back cover of your cookbook stating that your recipes have appeared in newspapers and food magazines. Besides, it's really fun to be published! It's a nice feeling to know that other people will enjoy your good cooking, even if you can't invite them personally into your kitchen.

Teach cooking classes through the adult continuing education program for your school district or at the community college. Not only will this give you professional status, you'll enjoy teaching others to cook and this is probably part of the reason you want to write a cookbook. In addition, you'll make some extra money which you can put toward your printing bill if you self-publish. This will also be a great sales avenue after your cookbook is published. Your students will eagerly and enthusiastically purchase your cookbook because they know you're a great cook and they want your recipes. They'll probably also buy lots of copies for their friends because they know the author.

Teaching cooking classes offers several other benefits. It will help you test your recipes and give you feedback to make sure they're perfect. Your students may supply you with some great recipes. It will give you extra confidence when you go out and personally promote your cookbook. Plus, you'll be a pro at cooking demonstrations.

Print Run, Pricing, and Profit

Figure the cost of publishing your cookbook at the outset and determine the size of your print run. How many cookbooks will you need to sell to turn a profit? How many people will buy your cookbook?

If you're shaky about how many cookbooks you think you can sell, it might be wise to do a test run, printing 200 to 500 cookbooks to see how well they sell. If they sell, you can go back to press for another printing. If they don't sell, you haven't put a lot of money into printing and you've gained valuable experience. Plus, you won't have thousands of cookbooks sitting in your garage getting moldy and mildewed.

While it's true that with a small print run the cookbook will cost a higher unit price, and a reprint will cost more than if you had ordered a larger quantity to begin with, it's best to err on the side of caution. You don't want to end up with a garage full of unsold cookbooks.

What should you charge for your cookbook? You want to do more than cover your expenses; you want to enjoy a healthy profit. What's a fair price that won't eat up your profits? You'll determine this based on similar cookbooks in the marketplace, the size and quality of your cookbook, and your COGS—Cost of Good Sold. COGS are the unit price for each cookbook.

For example, let's say your COGS are $2.00 for each cookbook. You decide to charge $10.00. That's an $8.00 profit, right? Yes and no. Yes, if you sell at full price. No, if you sell to bookstores and/or through a distributor.

Bookstores require a 40% discount off the cover price. Your $10.00 cookbook will give you a $6.00 profit, minus the $2.00

COGS, giving you a net profit of $4.00 per book. We're not done yet. You may have to pay shipping costs. Some bookstores will pay the freight; most won't. One cookbook, sent media mail, will cost you anywhere from $1.42 upwards, depending on the weight of your cookbook. Now you have a $2.58 profit or less. Factor in the cost of the shipping envelope and your other business expenses, and you may not have a profit at all. You might be losing money.

If you have a distributor to service bookstore accounts, they require a 55% discount. That leaves you with $4.50 minus the $2.00 COGS, which comes out to $2.50 per book profit. That's not pure profit. Figure in shipping costs to the distributor's warehouse. An average box of 30 cookbooks cost approximately $18.00 to ship by UPS if you have an account with them. If you don't have a UPS account, the shipping cost for the same box of cookbooks is $23.00. You do the math.

Your profit also has to cover the freebie cookbooks—where you won't be making any money at all—that you'll give away to book reviewers and the media, not to mention all the cookbooks you'll give as gifts to your friends and family. Consider all your other possible giveaways—the chefs who contributed recipes, advertisers who bought ad space, owners of local bookstores and retail stores to interest them in carrying your cookbook, the list goes on. Your profit margin also needs to figure in the cost of printing promotional materials, your start-up costs, and plenty of other extras to get the word out about your cookbook.

The price of your cookbook needs to cover all the related costs you will incur in printing and promoting it. You may think you'll have to charge $20.00 or $25.00 so it will pay its own way but this could be a big mistake. Keep in mind that your cookbook needs to be competitively priced. If your cover price is too high, no one will buy it. If your cover price is too low, you'll lose money on it.

Perceived value plays a big part here. If your cookbook looks professionally printed, it will command a higher price. People will pay a few dollars more for a cookbook that has attractive features, a great title, a four-color cover, eye-pleasing interior typesetting, and an interesting story line.

All these factors figure prominently in someone's decision to buy your cookbook. If you think you'll sell more copies if your cookbook has a lower price, you may find that people will think it's cheap and not buy it. Figure in all these considerations when you set the price for your cookbook. For the moment, set a tentative price. You'll set the final price when your cookbook is completed.

Beginning Your Budget

If you are self-publishing, you will be financing not only your start-up costs and the printing of your cookbook, but allocating funds for the promotion of it. There are lots of extras that will sneak up and bite you, eating away at your profits, if you haven't planned for them ahead of time.

Consider the cost of promotional materials you'll need to help get the word out about your cookbook. Perhaps you plan to have color flyers printed at the same time you print your cookbook. These 8-1/2 x 11 color glossies are also referred to as sell sheets. Another important selling tool is overrun book covers, which distributors will use to sell your cookbook to libraries and bookstores.

Other marketing materials might include recipe cards printed with a recipe on the front and your cookbook information on the back. You might want to print cookbook postcards; figure in the cost of stamps for mailing them. Refrigerator magnets are a great advertising tool. You'll also be shipping copies of your cookbook. You already know you'll have to pay freight but you'll have to buy padded mailing envelopes, too.

Do you plan to have posters printed and put them on bulletin boards around town? Figure in the cost of gas and thumbtacks. Take into account the cost of food for cooking demonstrations you plan to do, plus plates, napkins, and plastic utensils so people won't have to eat with their fingers.

You may be thinking at this point that your cookbook will be a labor of love and not much more, but don't despair. While it's true that your cookbook is a labor of love—you wouldn't do it otherwise—even publishing a cookbook at a loss offers you many advantages. It elevates you to the status of a professional—as an expert in your field—and can generate additional avenues of income. You will be asked to speak at food functions, earning you a nice speaker's fee. You can channel your cookbook into a catering business or catapult yourself as a cookbook consultant. Best of all, you'll be a published author; people will sit up and take notice of that. The icing on the cake is that a commercial publisher may be interested in your cookbook if you sell thousands of copies.

Don't think it will be impossible to make a profit. This isn't true. You know what your cookbook is worth and what it means to you. While all the up-front money comes out of your pocket to begin with, and there are no guarantees you'll make a profit on your investment, there are ways to turn the table. Having a quality product, and aggressively marketing and promoting your cookbook ensures a profit.

Some self-published cookbooks have sold well over 100,000 copies and gone into numerous printings. Other cookbooks serve the purpose of raising funds for a specific project and meet or exceed the expectations set out at the beginning. On the other side of the coin, there are some cookbooks that were lucky to sell even one hundred copies. The only guarantee in self-publishing is that your cookbook is published. Be realistic and positive in your projections. Your cookbook is more than recipes on paper bound into book form. Your cookbook is your baby; it's special and unique, a one-of-a-kind masterpiece.

Begin your budget by planning your promotions in the early stages of writing your cookbook. Decide how you want to market and sell your cookbook. Get quotes and prices for more than printing and promotional materials; determine how much you want to spend on getting the word out about your cookbook through direct mail, cooking demonstrations, and other avenues. You're serving a complete meal with your cookbook so be sure you're prepared with all the ingredients you will need.

Chapter Three

Vegetables & Side Dishes

Writing a cookbook is not much different than writing any other kind of book, except a cookbook needs to be very specific, consistent, and precise, with careful attention to detail. As with any book, you'll be writing an Introduction and front matter pages. With a cookbook, you'll be filling the chapters with more than recipes; you'll be including some special servings of side items.

A cookbook is so much more than a collection of recipes. Putting in a story line and weaving a theme throughout your cookbook pulls it all together. Adding extra items on the side will enhance your cookbook and add to its appeal and value. These special features will be a big selling attraction of your cookbook.

What do you want to serve on the side in your cookbook? What can you spice it up with to make it more enticing and a delicious read? Stories and anecdotes? Pithy sayings? Prep and cook times? Calorie counts? Nutritional analyses? Cooking hints and tips? Substitutions and serving suggestions? Presentations? Illustrations, clip art, borders, or food photography? What is going to give your cookbook its extra-special, taste-tempting appeal?

The fillers you choose to include will help to create healthy sales when your cookbook is published. Your mom always told you to eat your vegetables, that they were good for you and helped to make you healthy. Vegetables are an integral part of every meal; the side items you include in your cookbook will help bring in the green.

There are many side items you can serve in your cookbook which will enhance your recipes and make your cookbook more inviting and appetizing. Choose the items that fit well with your recipes and the theme of your cookbook, ones that will make your cookbook even more taste-tempting and appealing.

The following side items you might like to include in your cookbook are only suggestions and comprise a partial list. Look in lots of other cookbooks to see what they offer in the way of extra items. Pattern your cookbook in a similar way to the ones you think are visually attractive in style and design, and include the side items you think are appealing.

Headnotes could be your story line, the common thread that weaves throughout the chapters in your cookbook or headnotes could be an anecdote about preparing the recipe, food facts, or anything else you'd like to share. Headnotes are placed at the top of the recipe under the recipe title. The type is usually the same as the body of the recipe and is sometimes italicized.

Pithy Sayings are short quotes or little words of wisdom sprinkled throughout your cookbook that may or may not be related to food. They may be part of your story line. These are usually placed at the end of the recipe and are most often centered. The smaller type is in italics or enclosed with quote marks, sometimes both.

Culinary Clip Art is black and white line drawings of food and food related items. These look good on a page where the recipe doesn't fill the entire page. They help fill up the blank spaces and are eye-catching.

Other features, such as stylish borders also add visual appeal. Color photos of food add value to your cookbook and will up the cover price; however, they are extremely cost prohibitive unless you can sell at least 30,000 cookbooks to reach a break-even point.

Prep Time and **Cook Time** are placed either under the recipe title in smaller type to the right or the left, under the headnote, or sometimes at the bottom of the recipe. Prep time and cook time are exactly that. They show how long it takes to prepare the recipe and cook it.

It's nice to include these as a convenience for your readers. Someone may decide to make a recipe based on the time it takes and the time they have available, and they may not want to look through the recipe to determine the prep and cook times for themselves.

Number of Servings are either placed under the recipe title, centered, to the left or at the bottom of the recipe, and usually read 'Serves 4' or 'Makes 4 Servings.' The type, either italics or bold, is smaller. In recipes for cookies or muffins, use the word 'Yield' to signify the amount the recipe will provide.

Calorie Counts and/or a **Nutritional Analysis** are for weight-watchers, health-conscious people, and everyone else who wants to know these facts about their food. It's especially important to include them if you're writing a health-related cookbook, such as a low-carb or a low-fat diet cookbook. This information will be placed following the recipe, in smaller type and italicized. If you're going to include nutritional information, you must also include the number of servings. The nutritional information is preceded by 'per serving.'

There is nutritional analysis software available that will give you the correct computations for your recipes. You can Google 'nutritional analysis software' to find what you are looking for. A free trial version is offered at www.recipecalc.com.

Helpful Hints and **Cooking Tips** are additional information you want to include with the recipe to explain part of it or to simplify one of the steps, such as how to peel pearl onions so they will slip easily out of their skin or how to seed a tomato. These are usually placed after the recipe or in a sidebar.

Food Facts are interesting little tidbits of information about one of the ingredients. For example, in a recipe for *Blueberry Parfait*, you might want to say that blueberries have the highest amount of antioxidants of all fruits. Food facts are placed after the recipe or in a sidebar but occasionally make their way into a headnote.

Substitutions can be included in the list of ingredients or as a separate note after the recipe. If your recipe calls for '3 T. capers,' you can offer '3 T. green olives, chopped,' as an alternative. This is handy for cooks who may not have capers on hand, but have a cupboard full of olives. The recipe would be written, '3 T. capers or substitute 3 T. green olives, chopped.' The word 'substitute' may also be changed to 'use.'

Serving Suggestions are what you would suggest serving the recipe with. For example, with a recipe for meatloaf, you might suggest that mashed potatoes and buttered white corn would make a complete meal.

If you're writing a recipe for *Oriental Pepper Steak,* and you're going to say at the end of the recipe, 'Serve over a bed of rice,' be sure to include the amount of 'hot, cooked rice' in your ingredient list. Serving suggestions are placed at the end of the recipe, naturally following the order of things.

Variations are changing one or more ingredients that would make a different recipe. A recipe for *Chicken Pot Pie* could also be made into *Beef Pot Pie* by substituting beef for the chicken, changing one or two of the spices, and using beef gravy instead of chicken gravy. Use a variation only if a few ingredients are changed. If there are more than four changes, consider it to be a separate recipe. Variations follow the body of the recipe as a separate paragraph.

Optional Additions are items which may be included in the recipe for additional taste or to change the flavor or texture. For example, in a recipe for *Copper Canyon Chili,* you might want to say that red bell peppers could be added. Include optional additions in the list of ingredients with the word 'optional' in parentheses after the optional ingredient(s). In the cooking directions, include the optional ingredient with the words 'if using.'

I don't know about you, but optional additions are one of my pet peeves as far as recipes go. If the addition is optional, why include it? And if it enhances the taste and makes a better dish, why not include it in the ingredient list without the optional label attached to it? I'd much rather see a variation than an optional addition. But that's just my personal taste.

A **Presentation** shows how to serve the recipe with style and flair, make it visually appealing on the plate, and tantalize the eyes as well as the palate. This is different from a serving suggestion. Directions are provided for presenting the recipe with a garnish, listing the garnish ingredients in the recipe or telling how to arrange the food on the plate. A presentation is much more than 'slice across the grain' or 'serve hot.' It's what you would expect from a meal served in a restaurant. This is placed at the end of the recipe.

There are no hard and fast rules about where to place side items in your recipes, or what size pitch or font to use. Go with your imagination and creativity in designing the interior text of your cookbook. It's not a good idea to include all these side items with every recipe. It would make your recipe look too crowded, perhaps a little confusing and somewhat daunting.

When people look at the ingredient list in a recipe to decide if they want to make it, they also subconsciously notice if it looks too hard or complicated. Choose a few extra items that fit nicely into your cookbook; ones that will enhance your cookbook and add to its appeal. If you're including cook and prep times, and nutritional analyses, put them in every recipe.

Be consistent with the items you put in your cookbook, but also give yourself room to vary a bit. You don't need to include a head-note with every recipe but they look good scattered here and there, and make the text of your cookbook visually attractive and inviting. Your choice of side items to include will also be determined by how you plan to structure your cookbook and who you want it to appeal to.

Think about your favorite cookbooks. Why are they special to you? What do you like about them? What extra features and side items do they include that you find appealing and useful? How are they structured and formatted? How are the pages designed? What does the typesetting look like—font and pitch size?

Make your cookbook appealing to your reading and cooking audience. What can you include that will appeal to them? Make your cookbook special—one that will be used over and over.

The following recipes show different side items and formatting, to illustrate the extra items you might like to include with your recipes. Feel free to include any of these recipes in your cookbook and cite the source.

Wonderful Wine

This recipe is set block left. It includes a pithy saying, centered at the bottom, as well as a helpful hint. I discovered this recipe in a restaurant—The Ground Round. I asked for the recipe but they said it was a trade secret and wouldn't give it to me. Later, I worked there part-time and became friends with the bartender. She shared the recipe with me.

2 cups Rose wine
2 cups Burgundy wine
1 cup orange juice
1 cup lemonade
6 T. Grenadine
Crushed ice
Lemon, lime, and orange slices
Maraschino cherries

Mix the wines, orange juice, lemonade, and Grenadine together in a blender. Serve in wine glasses over crushed ice with a twist of lemon and lime, and an orange slice. Top each with a maraschino cherry.

Helpful Hint: This tastes a little like Kool-Aid but it's quite intoxicating.

> *"Cooking is like love. It should be entered into with abandon or not at all."*
>
> Harriet Van Horne

Dijon Chicken Bites

This recipe is set in a paragraph format for the instructions, which is the way recipes most often appear in cookbooks. The recipe title is centered; the ingredient list is block left. It contains a headnote, as well as a chef's tip and a presentation.

These "bites" are guaranteed to have your guests nibbling. It's best to double or triple the recipe.

1/4 cup butter
2 tsp. Dijon mustard
1 tsp. minced parsley
1 tsp. lemon juice
2 skinless, boneless chicken breasts,
   cut into 3/4-inch pieces
1/4 cup dry bread crumbs
1/4 cup Parmesan cheese
2 – 3 leaves green leaf lettuce
1/2 cup Dijon mustard
8 – 10 cherry tomatoes
8 – 10 green olives

Melt the butter in a 12-inch skillet over medium-high heat. Add the 2 T. mustard, parsley, and lemon juice, stirring quickly to mix.

Add the chicken to the skillet and sauté for 5 to 10 minutes or until the chicken is lightly browned and cooked through.

Sprinkle the chicken with the bread crumbs and Parmesan cheese. Toss lightly. Serve warm.

Chef's Tip: Cut the chicken while it is partially frozen. It will be easier to cut and the pieces will be uniform.

Presentation: Arrange the chicken on a platter lined with green leaf lettuce. Pierce each with a toothpick. Place a small serving bowl with 1/2 cup Dijon mustard in the middle. For color, add cherry tomatoes and green olives.

Curried Chicken Soup

Prep Time: 5 minutes
Cook Time: 1-1/2 hours

This recipe is formatted with a centered title, an indented, italicized ingredient list, and paragraph format for the instructions. You'll notice that all the ingredients are named rather than saying "add all ingredients." Sometimes prep time can be misleading. The following recipe calls for cooked chicken but doesn't incorporate the cooking time for the chicken in the recipe. It also doesn't suggest using a store-bought cooked chicken or canned cooked chicken, which would make the prep time accurate.

2 cups chopped, cooked chicken
1 (14.5 oz.) can tomatoes, cut up
1 tart apple, peeled and chopped
1/4 cup finely-chopped onion
1/4 cup chopped carrot
1/4 cup chopped celery
1 T. snipped parsley
2 tsp. lemon juice
1 tsp. curry powder
2 whole cloves
Salt and freshly ground black pepper to taste
2 chicken bouillon cubes
4 cups water

Place the cooked chicken, tomatoes, apple, onion, carrot, celery, parsley, lemon juice, curry powder, cloves, salt, pepper, bouillon cubes, and water in a 2-quart soup pan. Stir well to mix. Bring to a boil, then reduce the heat. Cover and simmer, stirring occasionally, for 1-1/2 hours. Remove the cloves before serving.

Special Spinach Burgers

Optional toppings are shown within the recipe, not as a separate item. There is also a suggestion for cooking these burgers in a different way.

1 (10 oz.) package frozen,
  chopped spinach
1/2 cup ricotta cheese
1 T. grated Parmesan cheese
2 pounds lean ground beef
1 medium egg, beaten
1/4 cup bread crumbs
4 seeded hamburger rolls or Kaiser buns

In a medium-size saucepan, cook the spinach according to package directions. Turn off the heat. Drain well, then return to the saucepan. Stir in the ricotta and Parmesan cheeses.

While the spinach is cooking, combine the ground beef, egg, and bread crumbs in a medium-size bowl. Shape into 8 patties.

Spread the spinach mixture on top of 4 of the patties to within 1/4-inch of the edge. Top with the remaining patties and seal the edges by tightly crimping them together with your fingers.

Brown the patties in a 12-inch skillet over medium-high heat. Serve on rolls with your choice of toppings, such as lettuce, tomato, cheese, sautéed onions and mushrooms, and/or crisp bacon slices. Or simply adorn with ketchup and mustard.

Suggestion: These burgers can also be grilled.

Chicken Asparagus Marsala
Makes 4 Servings · Net Carbs: 5g

The ingredient list in this recipe is indented and italicized. This recipe, from Delmarva Poultry Industry, shows you what you're getting in terms of calories, carbs, fat, fiber, protein, and other important information. I didn't change the ingredients but have modified the recipe a bit in terms of directions to make it clearer. This recipe also offers a substitution. Since this is a continued recipe and there is white space on the next page, culinary clip art has been added.

> *4 skinless, boneless chicken breasts*
> *2 T. butter*
> *1 (8 oz.) container button mushrooms, quartered*
> *1/4 cup Marsala wine*
> *1/4 cup water*
> *1/2 tsp. salt*
> *1/4 tsp. freshly ground black pepper*
> *1 pound fresh asparagus, cut into 5-inch spears (or*
> * use 1-1/2 (10 oz.) packages frozen asparagus spears)*
> *1 T. chopped fresh parsley*

Place the chicken between two sheets of plastic wrap. Flatten to 1/4-inch thickness with a meat mallet.

Place the butter in a 12-inch skillet over medium-high heat.

When the butter melts and begins to sizzle, add the chicken and cook, turning, about 5 minutes on each side or until browned. Remove the chicken and set aside.

Add the mushrooms to the skillet and cook, stirring, about 2 minutes.

Add the wine, water, salt, and pepper. Stir.

Return the chicken to the pan. Spoon the sauce over the chicken.

Arrange the asparagus spears over the chicken. Heat to boiling, then reduce the heat to medium. Cover and cook about 8 minutes or until the chicken is cooked through and the asparagus is tender.

Transfer the chicken and asparagus to a serving platter and keep warm.

Heat the wine sauce to boiling, then let boil for about 2 minutes to reduce the liquid.

Spoon the wine sauce over the chicken and asparagus. Sprinkle with chopped parsley.

Per serving: 236 cal, 31g pro, 8g carbs, 3g fiber, 8g fat, 3g sat fat, 68 mg chol, 424 mg sod

This recipe could be made even better by including a helpful hint about how to break the asparagus at the flex point to eliminate the tough, woody part. Another way to improve it would be to explain that reducing the wine sauce increases its flavor. If someone has never made a wine sauce reduction, he or she might think there's going to be less sauce for the chicken and may omit this flavorful step.

The recipe originally called for '1 cup mushrooms.' This leaves a lot to the imagination. What kind of mushrooms? Button, cremini, portabello, porcini, or some other kind? Are they to be sliced, diced, chopped, quartered, or left whole? Be specific with all the ingredients you include in your recipe. Keep in mind that this may be someone's first venture into the kitchen. Write your recipe accordingly.

Sun-Dried Tomato Chicken

The title and ingredient list are centered and italicized; the instructions are indented and numbered, shown in a paragraph format. This recipe is not only delicious, it contains a helpful hint in the form of a chef's tip, as well as a headnote and a professional presentation.

This dish offers layers of flavor with a hint of sunshine and a touch of red wine. You'll savor the delectable taste in every bite.

1/4 cup coarsely chopped sun-dried tomatoes
1/2 cup chicken broth, hot
1/2 cup sliced button mushrooms
2 medium green onions, chopped
2 cloves garlic, finely chopped
2 T. dry red wine
1 tsp. olive oil
4 skinless, boneless chicken breasts
1/2 cup milk
2 tsp. cornstarch
1/2 tsp. dried basil
2 cups hot cooked fettuccine, tossed with 2 T. olive
oil and sprinkled with fresh chopped parsley

1. Mix the tomatoes and hot broth in a small bowl. Let stand for 30 minutes for the tomatoes to rehydrate.

2. Cook the mushrooms, onions, and garlic in wine in a 12-inch nonstick skillet over medium heat for about 3 minutes, stirring occasionally, until the mushrooms are tender. Remove the mixture from the skillet and set aside.

3. Increase the heat to medium high. Add the oil to the skillet. When the oil is hot, add the chicken and brown it on both sides.

4. Add the tomato mixture. Heat to boiling, then reduce the heat to low. Cover and simmer for 10 to 15 minutes, stirring occasionally. Remove the chicken and keep warm.

5. In a small bowl, mix the milk, cornstarch, and basil together. Stir this mixture into the tomato mixture in the skillet. Heat to boiling, stirring constantly. Boil and stir for 1 minute.

6. Return the mushroom mixture to the skillet and heat through.

Chef's Tip: Use kitchen scissors to snip the sun-dried tomatoes into small pieces before soaking them in liquid.

Presentation: Spread the cooked fettuccine on an oval platter. Overlap the chicken breasts on the pasta and spoon the mushroom sauce over.

Monday Night Meatloaf

This recipe has a ragged right margin (not justified). Since it is rather short, it fits nicely after the longer recipe which had to be carried over to another page. It is formatted with title and ingredient list flush left; the instructions are indented. A sans serif font was used, making it more difficult on the eyes to read. The recipe itself is pretty basic and straightforward, and is also pretty blah. This recipe can be made even better by offering a variation. There's also a helpful hint here.

2 pounds lean ground beef
1 small onion, chopped
2 slices bread, crumbled
1 medium egg, slightly beaten
2/3 cup milk
1 (8 oz.) can tomato sauce
Salt and black pepper to taste

Preheat the oven to 350 degrees.

In a medium-size bowl, combine the ground beef, onion, bread crumbs, egg, milk, tomato sauce, salt, and pepper. Mix well and shape into an oval loaf. Place into a meatloaf tin and bake for one hour.

Variation: To make *Mexican Meatloaf*, substitute 1 cup salsa for the tomato sauce. Use crushed tortilla chips instead of the bread crumbs.

Helpful Hint: Line the bottom and sides of the meatloaf tin with aluminum foil. The cleanup is much easier.

Lentil Soup with Ham

This recipe provides interesting food facts—tidbits of information about lentils. You'll also notice that the methodology is a bit chatty and conversational, as if the cook is in the kitchen with you.

1 (1-pound) bag of lentils
2 large carrots, sliced
2 stalks celery, thinly sliced
1-1/2 tsp. dried basil
1 ham bone (smoked)
1-1/2 cups ham, cubed
1-1/2 cups minced onion
3 tsp. salt
1 tsp. black pepper
1-1/2 tsp. dried marjoram
8 cups water (or less)
1/4 cup sherry
Croutons
Grated Parmesan cheese

Wash and drain the lentils in a colander, picking them over for stones and debris.

Place the lentils in a large saucepan. Add the carrots, celery, basil, ham bone, ham, onion, salt, pepper, marjoram, and water. For a thicker broth, use a little less water. Cover and bring to a boil. Reduce the heat and cook just under a boil for 3 hours, stirring often.

The soup is done when the lentils are soft and the flavors have blended. Just before serving, add the sherry and stir well.

Serve the soup in individual bowls. Sprinkle with croutons and grated Parmesan cheese.

Food Facts: Lentils are richer in protein than any other legumes except soybeans. Most lentils do not need soaking before cooking. Red or split orange lentils are quick-cooking, making them useful for thickening curries, stews, or casseroles.

Yogurt Chicken

This recipe has a centered, italicized title, the ingredient list is indented, and the instructions are set off with a bullet. It offers several alternatives if you don't have the ingredient on hand or if you simply want to change the taste. It also offers a chef's tip and a presentation.

2 – 3 T. butter
1 cup coarsely chopped onions
4 skinless, boneless chicken breasts
1 cup plain yogurt
Salt and freshly ground black pepper to taste
1/4 tsp. allspice
1/4 tsp. cumin
1/4 tsp. cardamon
2 fresh tomatoes, chopped (or
  1 (14.5 oz.) can diced tomatoes)
2 cups hot cooked white rice
Sprigs of fresh parsley

◆ In a 12-inch skillet, melt the butter over medium heat. Add the onions and sauté until they are caramelized. Remove and set aside.

◆ Add the chicken to the skillet and brown on both sides.

◆ Return the onions to the pan. Add the yogurt, salt, pepper, allspice, cumin, cardamon, and tomatoes. Reduce the heat, cover and simmer for 1 hour, stirring once or twice.

Substitutions: Use lamb or beef instead of chicken.

Chef's Tip: Caramelize means to brown.

Presentation: Place a bed of rice on a serving platter. Spread the chicken breasts on top, overlapping them a bit, and pour the sauce over. Garnish with sprigs of parsley.

Centered Sausage

The recipe title is centered and set in a different font from the directions; ingredients are shown in a side-by-side format. The serving suggestion is centered at the bottom of the recipe. A serving suggestion is an item or items that will go well with the prepared recipe. One of my friends invited me over to dinner and made this recipe. After the first bite, I begged her for the recipe. She served this meal with mashed potatoes and green beans. You'll notice in this recipe that a brand name is included. If a brand name is vital to the recipe, include it, otherwise let your readers choose the brands they normally buy.

1-1/2 pounds lean ground beef	Dash cloves
1 cup finely chopped, unpeeled apple	1 package Brown 'n Serve
1/3 cup diced onion	Original Flavor sausage links
1 medium egg	2 – 3 T. olive oil
1 tsp. salt	2 T. flour
1/4 tsp. black pepper	1 beef bouillon cube
1/4 tsp. cinnamon	1 cup water

🍽 In a large mixing bowl, combine the ground beef, apple, onion, egg, salt, pepper, cinnamon, and cloves. Divide the mixture into 10 equal parts. Mold each part around a sausage link, sealing the ends.

🍽 Heat the oil in a 12-inch skillet over medium heat. Add the meat and brown on all sides. Remove and set aside.

🍽 Drain the fat from the skillet, reserving just enough to cover the bottom of the skillet. Stir the flour into the fat. Cook over low heat, stirring constantly until the mixture is smooth and bubbly.

🍽 Add the bouillon cube and water. Heat to boiling, stirring constantly until the bouillon cube is dissolved and the gravy has thickened.

🍽 Reduce the heat to medium-low. Return the meat to the skillet. Cover and simmer for 15 minutes.

Serving Suggestion: Serve with mashed potatoes and green beans.

Apple Bread Bake

This entire recipe is centered and italicized. Optional additions are a bit like variations and substitutions, except optional items are offered in the ingredient list or at the end as a separate note to add the item or items to the basic recipe.

Butter for the baking dish
1 cup bread crumbs
3 T. butter, softened
1 tsp. grated orange zest
1/2 cup sugar
1 tsp. cinnamon
1/3 cup raisins
1/3 cup chopped walnuts (optional)
4 medium apples, peeled and thinly sliced
1/4 cup apple juice
Cool Whip

Preheat the oven to 375 degrees.
Lightly butter a 9 x 9 baking dish. Set aside.

In a medium-size bowl, mix together the bread crumbs,
3 T. butter, orange zest, sugar, and cinnamon.

Add the raisins, and walnuts if using, to the bread crumb mixture.

Place half the sliced apples in the prepared baking dish.
Cover with half the bread crumb mixture. Repeat.

Pour the apple juice evenly over the top. Bake for 45 minutes.

Serve warm with a dollop of whip cream.

Note: The ingredient list in the original recipe didn't start off with 'Butter for the baking dish.' When I first read the recipe, it occurred to me that people might think the '3 T. butter' was what was supposed to be used to butter the baking dish. The addition I made to the ingredient list clarifies this.

Pepper Beef Roulades

The ingredient list is shown in three parts; the divisions are bolded and set in a different font than the ingredient list and instructions; this is also done in the body of the recipe. This recipe features a headnote and a professional presentation. Dress up your recipes by showing how to serve them in style. This recipe also offers an optional addition contained within the recipe directions instead of in the ingredient list or at the end.

Don't let the long list of ingredients scare you off. This recipe is quite simple to prepare and is worth the time it takes. This spectacular meal offers varied tastes in each bite. It's a feast for your mouth.

Roulades —

12 (2 ounce) slices top round
Salt, freshly ground black pepper, and paprika
Mustard and ketchup as needed
1 red bell pepper, cut into thin julienne strips
1 cup pickles, cut into thin julienne strips
1 pound bacon, crisp-cooked and coarsely chopped
1 large onion, diced and cooked with the bacon
1/2 cup butter, melted

Braising Sauce —

2 T. olive oil
1/3 cup chopped onions
1/3 cup chopped carrots
1/3 cup chopped celery
1 tsp. tomato paste
2 T. flour
1/4 cup dry red wine
6 cups beef broth
Salt and freshly ground black pepper

Garnish —

2 T. butter
1 (8 oz.) container button mushrooms, quartered
1 small red bell pepper, cut into thin julienne strips
1/2 cup coarsely chopped pickles

2 carrots, coarsely chopped
Freshly ground black pepper
1/2 tsp. dried fines herbes
Fresh parsley sprigs

Preheat the oven to 400 degrees.

Roulades: With a meat mallet, flatten the slices until they are about 1/4-inch thick. Season the meat slices with salt, pepper, and paprika. Smear the meat slices with mustard and ketchup.

Place an equal amount of the red bell peppers, pickles, bacon, and onions on each meat slice. Roll up the slices and secure them with large wooden toothpicks. Place the roulades in a roasting pan and coat them with the melted butter. Cook for 30 minutes or until evenly browned.

Braising Sauce: While the beef is in the oven, heat the oil in a 12-inch skillet over medium-high heat. Add the onion, carrots, and celery. Sauté until tender, about 10 minutes.

Add the tomato paste. Cook for 1 minute, stirring.

Add the flour and stir until well blended.

Add the wine, stirring well and scraping up the browned bits from the bottom of the skillet.

Add the broth and bring the mixture to a boil. Let boil for 2 minutes.

Remove the pan from the oven and reduce the heat to 250 degrees. Pour the braising sauce over the roulades in the roasting pan. Cover the pan with aluminum foil and return it to the oven. Cook for 2 hours, turning the roulades occasionally.

Remove the pan from the oven. Transfer the beef roulades to a warm serving platter. Remove the toothpicks. Cover with aluminum foil to keep warm.

Strain the sauce into a medium-size saucepan. Bring to a boil over high heat, then reduce the heat to low. Simmer until the sauce thickens, about 10 to 12 minutes. Season to taste with salt and pepper. (If desired, 2 cups heavy cream may be added to this sauce during the last 5 minutes of simmering.)

Garnish: While this is cooking, melt the butter in a 12-inch skillet over medium heat. Sauté the mushrooms, red bell pepper, pickles, and carrots until tender-crisp, about 8 to 10 minutes. Season with freshly ground black pepper and dried fines herbes.

Presentation: Spread a small amount of the sauce on a dinner plate in a swirling circle. Arrange 2 roulades in the center and pour some sauce over them. Garnish with sautéed mushrooms, red bell pepper strips, pickles, carrots, and a sprig or two of fresh parsley.

Chapter Four

Main Dishes

Now you're into the meat of the matter. Writing your recipes is a matter of taste. Flavor your words to make them mouth-watering. Find the format that works for you. Do the details with a religious fervor. Consistency counts. Being consistent with all your recipes will give your cookbook continuity and cohesiveness; it will help your readers enjoy cooking from your cookbook and to come back for second helpings.

Make sure your recipes offer really good, taste-tempting, mouth-watering meals that are nicely presented, written clearly, and are easy to follow. If you've ever read a poorly-written recipe or one that was confusing, you know how turned off it makes you feel. After talking to or maybe screaming at the recipe, saying things like, "Whaaaat!?" or "That can't be right" or "That's really gross," you throw the cookbook down in disgust, vowing to never use it again. Don't do this to your readers. Offer them easy-to-follow recipes they'll want to make.

When people read a recipe, they imagine what the finished dish will look like, smell like, and taste like. Write your recipes to inspire the reader's imagination, to engage their mind, their senses, and especially their taste buds. Make the wording of your recipes so visually delicious that the reader can see the finished product, smell the aroma, and taste it just by reading your recipe.

Writing Recipes

Assume your reader is a novice cook and this is his or her first venture into the kitchen. Make your recipes clear and easy to follow. Use visual cues, such as 'cook until brown' or 'cheese is bubbly' or 'cake is done when it pulls away from the side of the pan.' Think about your first ventures, or misadventures, in the kitchen and how your mother or someone else mentored you, showing you how to cook and prepare meals.

Create a conversation. Make your readers feel as if you are in the kitchen, showing them how to prepare the food and helping them follow the recipe. Do this in the directions. Talk to the cook as if you are there, looking over his or her shoulder, explaining how to make the recipe, offering your ideas, guidance, and expertise. Be clear and specific.

Don't complicate the instructions for making a recipe by showing off your expertise. While you may know what a comal is, your reader might not. Show off your expertise by clearly explaining everything. You're not only a cookbook author, you're a teacher, helping home cooks learn how to prepare your recipes so they turn out as delicious as when you prepare them. By the way, a comal is a round, low-sided skillet similar to a griddle which is used to cook tortillas on. You can include additional information such as this in a note after your recipe. Cooks love to learn new things that will enhance and expand their culinary repertoire.

If you're going to use a lot of terms, or even a few, which might be unfamiliar to some of your readers, it's a good idea to include a glossary or to explain the terms when they appear in the recipes. Keep in mind that many people only have a basic knowledge of food preparation and cooking. Write your recipes accordingly.

For example, several years ago I saw a recipe for *Celery Root au Gratin*. I thought that celery root is what was at the bottom of the stalk of celery. The recipe grossed me out. I always cut the bottom part off and threw it away. To me, it was garbage. I logically concluded that the recipe was garbage. It wasn't until much later, when I was reading another cookbook that offered a recipe for *Celery Root Soup*, that I discovered what celery root really is.

Want to know what it is? Maybe you already know. Celery root is a round, hairy, knob-like vegetable that varies in size. It has a mild, delicate taste; when cooked, its texture is creamy. It is available in the produce section from fall through early spring. The best way to peel celery root is with a paring knife.

Write all your recipes in the same format. Be consistent. If your ingredients are indented block left under the recipe title and your instructions follow in paragraphs, use this same format for all your recipes. It's confusing to your reader if you vary this; it also makes your cookbook look scattered and haphazard.

List the ingredients in your recipe in the order they will be used. If your recipe contains a long list of ingredients, break them up, if you can, into smaller segments. This makes your recipe look user-friendly and is easier to follow. You might also want to include a headnote explaining the recipe. (See *Pepper Beef Roulades* in the previous chapter.)

Pay attention to detail. Consistency counts. Decide if you will use abbreviations or spell everything out. Are you going to write '1 cup flour' or '1 C. flour,' or '1 T. butter' vs. '1 tablespoon butter?' Speaking of butter, 1/2 cup butter doesn't change somewhere in your cookbook to 1 stick butter. Use the same abbreviations or spelling for every recipe.

Be specific when giving can sizes. '1 can diced tomatoes' will have your readers wondering what size can to use. Write the ingredient this way: '1 (14.5 oz.) can diced tomatoes.' Also clarify if the ingredient is to be used with the juice or without the juice. Either say 'with juice' or 'drained.'

The same follows for container sizes. If you write '1 container mushrooms,' specify the container size, what type of mushrooms, and whether the mushrooms are whole, sliced, diced, quartered, or chopped. Make everything very clear and specific for your readers.

Many people who are experienced cooks and culinary artists, cook by feel. A dash of this and a pinch of that may be how you create your kitchen masterpieces, but your dash or pinch in a recipe may be a handful to someone else. Always give exact measurements. It will inspire confidence in an inexperienced cook. Sooner or later, they'll graduate to dashes and pinches, and wonder why they ever had to measure anything.

Another way to clarify the ingredients in your recipes is to offer approximations when needed. '1/2 cup lime juice' can be further clarified by adding 'about 4 limes' in parentheses.

Specify sizes of ingredients. Does the recipe call for an egg? Tell your reader what size. If there's an onion in the recipe, it is white, yellow, green, or red? Is it small, medium, or large? If the recipe calls for a specific type of onion, such as Bermuda, Spanish, or pearl onions, be sure to specify the onion to be used.

Sometimes directions for the preparation of food are given in the ingredient list rather than in the directions. For example, '1 cup onions, coarsely chopped' or '6 slices bacon, crisp-cooked and crumbled.' Instructions in the ingredient list help the cook know what food to prep beforehand. Plus, it makes the recipe look shorter because the directions aren't in the body; therefore, the recipe looks easier.

If the same ingredient will be used in two different parts of the recipe, list it in the ingredient list either once, '4 T. butter, divided' or in the order it will be used, '2 T. butter.' Further down the list of ingredients where it will be used in the recipe, list it again, '2 T. butter.' Either way is fine. It's a matter of your personal taste and preference. If you choose divided use, be sure to show it appropriately in your cooking methodology by saying 'add the 2 T. butter' instead of 'add the butter.'

When naming cooking utensils, always use the same text. A 12-inch skillet doesn't magically change into a large skillet from one recipe to the next if the recipe needs a 12-inch skillet. If your recipe calls for a saucepan to be used, specify the quart size. You want your readers to use the equivalent of the same kitchen equipment you use in your recipes to get the same results, so let them know the proper pans and utensils to use. Keep in mind what cooking equipment is in the average kitchen.

Always be consistent in your directions. If you say, 'Brown the meat in a 12-inch skillet over medium-high heat,' then say that in every recipe that applies. Don't change to, 'In a 12-inch skillet over medium-high heat, brown the meat.'

Make your recipes easy to read. Be consistent with your commas in every recipe. Proper grammar and punctuation count. For example, 'salt, pepper, cumin, and oregano' as opposed to 'salt, pepper, cumin and oregano.' Decide what style to use and stick with it.

In your directions, name the ingredients that will be added in each step. Don't say, 'add all the herbs and spices' or 'add the next five ingredients.' It's irritating to have to double-check the ingredient list, plus it makes your recipe confusing. It's better to say, 'add the oregano, thyme, garlic salt, and black pepper.' Be clear as to what goes in at every step of the recipe.

If your recipe calls for two types of pepper, such as red pepper and black pepper, specify in your directions which pepper to use. If you simply say 'add the pepper,' the cook isn't going to know which pepper to add and will have to read the ingredient list again to see which pepper needs to be added first. This also holds true for red, green, and yellow bell peppers.

It's best for complete recipes to be on one page. Some recipes will be short and won't take up an entire page. Putting two short recipes on the same page, with space between them, looks good. Inserting food-related clip art or short sayings to take up the empty space is another option.

Other recipes will be too long for one page and will have to be continued on to the next page. Try to put them on facing pages so your readers can follow the recipe easily. If your reader has to keep flipping back and forth between pages, he or she might think your recipe is too much trouble. And, as we all know, cooking can be a little messy. Do you want your cookbook to end up with smudges of flour and butter, or splatters of tomato sauce on the pages?

Use paragraphs for the directions, also known as the methodology. Write clearly in complete sentences. A lot of recipes are written in phrases; they are jumpy and jumbled. Cookbooks that present their recipes in complete sentences are easier to read and follow. It feels as if the cookbook author is talking with the reader, explaining how to make the recipe every step of the way.

Don't make the mistake of writing all the directions in one paragraph. This makes the recipe seem hard and complicated, much too difficult to follow and too much trouble to make. It's easy to skip over something, and having to find your place in the recipe directions time and time again for each step is aggravating. Cookbooks where the directions are in separate paragraphs for each step of the process are much more user-friendly and inviting. Perhaps you'll want to set off the step-by-step instructions with a number, a bullet, or culinary clip art.

Think about the cookbooks you really enjoy because the recipes are clear and every step is explained. Model your cookbook the same way. Present all your recipes and non-recipe content in a consistent format that is well written and easy to follow. Make your cookbook user-friendly.

Typesetting Recipes

No matter how good your recipes are, cooks won't be tempted to make them, or even buy your cookbook, if the interior text and page layout aren't eye-pleasing, inviting, and appealing. Serving your cookbook with style says that you care about the recipes in your cookbook. Readers will pick up on that subconsciously. Style and design your cookbook in an appealing manner by choosing the page layout and interior typestyles that will compliment your cookbook.

It's easy to typeset your cookbook. Preparing camera-ready copy, which means the printer will print your cookbook exactly the way your hard copy looks, gives you a lot of flexibility with the typestyles and additional items you wish to include. You can also submit your cookbook press-ready by sending a disk with your fonts and formatting embedded, and you can go one step further by submitting your cookbook as a PDF (Portable Document File). All the printer has to do is run your file.

If you're going with a commercial publisher, they will do all the typesetting and numerous other items, including choosing the format and font, arranging the recipes in your cookbook, selecting the interior design, and choosing the binding.

If you are self-publishing, you have a world of choices. It's fun to make your cookbook as unique and individual as you are. It's almost as much fun to express yourself with creating and styling your cookbook as it is to cook. Look at professional cookbooks to see how they're styled. This will give you lots of great ideas. It will help you in choosing how to style your cookbook and in selecting the additional items you want to include.

A few words about fonts: Use a serif font, one with feet, such as Times New Roman or Garamond, 11 or 12-pitch. The type is easier to read and your readers will thank you for that. If your pitch is too small, or if the font is difficult to read, your readers may get bleary-eyed trying to follow your recipes.

There are several fonts you might like to use for your recipes. Some script fonts look like normal handwriting, are easy on the eyes, and easy to read. It makes a cookbook look and feel more natural and homey, adding kind of a kitchen table, personal touch. But beware of script fonts like Snell Roundhand and Bradley Hand because they're too light, look like calligraphy, and are hard to read. Also watch out for Smudger and Viner Hand. They're difficult to read because they're jagged and sharp. That's not the impression you want to give about your recipes.

Use only two, perhaps three, different fonts for your recipe title, recipe directions, and any additional items you plan to include. More than three can cause the same bleary-eyed effect. If your readers have a hard time reading your recipes because of the font and pitch, or because of too many different typestyles, they'll subconsciously think your recipes are too difficult to follow. They may make this decision in the bookstore with your cookbook in hand. Bleary-eyed in the bookstore equals putting your cookbook back on the shelf, not buying it and taking it home into their kitchen.

Make your recipe title bold, 13 or 14-pitch. Use a sans serif font, one without feet. This makes your recipe title stand out and be noticed. Tahoma, Helvetica, Arial, and Century Gothic are good fonts for recipe titles, as well as some script fonts. Experiment with fonts and pitch; find a happy medium. Use fonts that look good with your recipes, ones that make your cookbook look inviting and user-friendly.

Make your cookbook eye-pleasing and easy to read by opening the space between the lines. A single-spaced recipe is a bit difficult to read and will cause eye strain. A one-and-one-half spaced recipe is too much space. A double-spaced recipe looks like a draft of your cookbook. Typeset your recipes using the raised spacing on your computer. Justify the paragraphs that you use for the cooking methodology.

You have many choices and options in how you want to style your recipes. You may want to center the title and list of ingredients, then do the directions in paragraph form. You may want to italicize the recipe title and ingredients, then do straight type for the directions. Still another choice is to list your ingredients in two columns, then do the methodology in paragraphs set off by bullets or culinary clip art. The two-column format for the ingredient list will save page space, but also tends to make your recipes look crowded and a bit confusing.

You may want to do the recipe title and ingredients flush left, then do the directions in paragraph format. Or you may want to center the recipe title and block indent the ingredient list. Or you might like to style your cookbook in a side-by-side format with the ingredients on the left side and a smaller left margin, and the directions on the right with a wider margin. Or, in the same format, list your ingredients and methodology on the left side with a wider margin and insert notes and side items on the shorter right side.

Beware the all-in-one paragraph format. It's too confusing to prep and follow the recipe. All the ingredients, typed in bold, are listed within the directions. This might be okay if it's a short recipe that calls for only two or three ingredients.

Look at lots of cookbooks to see how the recipes are typeset and formatted, then choose a style that is appealing to you. Once you make your choice, be consistent. Every recipe should be set up the same way.

If you decide to publish your cookbook with one of the cookbook printers listed in Appendix A, you can either typeset your cookbook and submit it camera-ready or press-ready, or submit your recipes, either typed or handwritten, and they will do the typesetting for you, using one of their recipe formats. This limits your choices as to how you want the interior of your cookbook to look, though you will get to choose one of their recipe styles.

Most of the cookbook printers offer online submission, using their software at their website. This is convenient, doing everything on the Internet, but if you want your cookbook to be individual and unique, it's best to typeset it yourself and send the printer either a camera-ready copy—your hard copy with instructions or a press-ready copy—your hard copy for proofing purposes and either a CD or a disk of your typeset cookbook or a PDF on a CD or disk.

If you go with a cookbook printer's recipe format, their margins—left, right, top, and bottom—are fairly small, one-half inch or less. The recipes are all one paragraph and usually continue on to the next page. Your recipes will be crowded and crammed; you'll end up with less pages and you'll spend less money on your printing bill. If you want your cookbook to be eye-pleasing and easy to follow, do your own typesetting. Include white space and write your recipes in step-by-step paragraphs. Make your margins one inch all around, leaving a left gutter margin of 1/4-inch for the binding.

You have several options in choosing the cover and binding for your cookbook. You can select soft or hard cover with comb or wire binding, plastic coil, concealed wire, wire wrap-around, a 3-ring binder, or perfect bound. All these bindings except perfect bound, allow your cookbook to open flat for ease of cooking preparation. A perfect bound book is a trade paper book, which most libraries and many bookstores prefer.

If you plan to sell to libraries and bookstores, be aware that libraries are hesitant to buy cookbooks that aren't perfect bound or concealed wire, but might be willing to buy a cookbook with comb binding if it looks professional and the title, author, and publisher are imprinted on the spine. Bookstores are a bit more lenient, but they won't buy a 3-ring binder cookbook unless it is shrink wrapped. That sort of defeats your purpose in writing a cookbook. People won't be able to look through it at the bookstore to see if your recipes are ones they would enjoy preparing.

Divider pages divide the chapters in your cookbook by food group. They list the title of the chapter, such as Appetizers & Beverages, Main Dishes, and Desserts. You can go with the pre-printed, four-color dividers—which are coordinated with the cover—that the cookbook printers offer. Or you can create your own with the chapter title you choose, perhaps listing the recipes by name that are included in that chapter, or writing a paragraph or two relative to that section of your cookbook. Some divider pages have tabs; these look good in the 3-ring binders.

If you go with what the printer offers, you will have to live with their divider pages to describe the recipes in each section. One way around this is to prepare your own subheadings if you typeset your cookbook and insert them in the text of your cookbook where appropriate. For example, in the Main Dishes section, you might like to separate your recipes into Meat, Poultry, and Seafood instead of letting the cookbook printer lump them all together.

Since your dividers will all start on a right page, be sure you have enough recipes in the previous section to go all the way to the last, left page. You don't want to end up with a blank page. Just put another recipe or two into that section.

Present your pages professionally. Place running heads with page numbers on each page. Running heads are the title of the cookbook on left pages and the name of each chapter on right pages. Running heads can be either centered or placed flush right and left (for right and left pages). Century Gothic or Arial, 9 or 10-pitch, is a nice typestyle to use. Running heads should be 1/2-inch down from the top of the page.

Your page numbers can be centered on the bottom of the page for the first page of a chapter, 1/2-inch up from the bottom and placed flush left and right at the top if your running heads are centered, or separated by several spaces if your running heads are flush left and right. Page numbers look lonely all by themselves; you might want to include a little flourish with them, perhaps adding a small clip art or an extended hyphen before and after the number.

You can have your recipes inked in black, blue, green, red, or brown. Black is the standard, but you can opt for another color if you'd like. Some cookbooks incorporate two colors, such as green and brown. Most cookbooks are printed on white paper; cream paper is also available.

Putting Your Cookbook Together

Assembling your cookbook follows an established order. Front matter is what goes in the front pages before the main body of the book, thus it is called front matter. The title page, which contains the title and subtitle, comes first, nicely centered somewhere in the upper middle of the page. The author's name is centered in the lower part of the page. The name of the publisher, and the city and state of the publisher goes at the bottom of the page.

Directly behind that page is the verso page, which is printed on a left page (on the back of the title page). The verso page shows the title, subtitle, year of copyright, author, ISBN, LC number or CIP, publisher name and address, website, and any other vital information pertaining to your cookbook.

After that comes the Dedication page, and any other pages you'd like to include, such as an Acknowledgements page or an About the Author page, that will precede the main body of your cookbook. These are all placed beginning on right pages. They are usually one page. If they carry over to another page, they are placed on the back, left page. Next comes your Table of Contents and an Introduction.

Supplementary information which will enhance your cookbook and is relative to the theme, goes in a separate chapter or two in the front of your cookbook, placed either before or after the Introduction. For example, health-related cookbooks usually include a diet program and a chapter or two on that particular diet. A barbecue cookbook may describe different kinds of grills. A vegetarian cookbook might describe every vegetable that exists.

Some cookbooks offer a suggested list of menus showing recipes, along with the page number for those recipes, that go well together to make a meal or for a party. Sometimes these are shown on the divider pages but are most often placed in the front of the book. If you're doing a cookbook that is centered around dinner parties or theme parties, adding menus or meal suggestions would be a great idea. Otherwise, let your readers determine for themselves what dishes go well with each other or give suggestions in your recipes.

Some of your supplementary information could be considered back matter. For example, Tex-Mex cookbooks usually include an explanatory list of chile peppers and a resource guide listing places to buy them.

After front matter, and any supplementary information, comes the body of your cookbook—your chapters with recipes, story line, and any other information that will be included with your recipes. Chapters follow the natural progression of a meal, and are set off by dividers or chapter pages.

On to back matter, which is placed after your recipes. An index is the alphabetized list of recipe titles. There are several ways to do an index. One is alphabetical by recipe title. Another way lists all the recipes alphabetically and is also cross-referenced by main ingredient, followed by the title of the recipe. A third way is to list the recipes alphabetically under the appropriate chapter name.

Inserts and supplementary information can be placed either after the index or just before it. Inserts are items relative to cooking but not directly related to the recipes. These can include, but are not limited to: A calorie chart, a list of herbs and spices, cooking terms, and an equivalency or substitution chart. Most of the cookbook printers offer an optional insert either free or for a minimal charge. If the pre-printed insert enhances and adds to the value of your cookbook, go for it. If it's just extra pages and doesn't fit the theme of your cookbook, it's best to omit them.

Last, but not least, you may want to include an order form at the end of your cookbook. If you plan to only sell to your local community, an order form is a good idea. An order form provides an easy way for people to order extra copies of your cookbook. Include lines for their name and address. Show the price of your cookbook, any tax that must be paid, the shipping and handling charges, who to make the check payable to, and the address to send the check to.

Commercial cookbooks don't include an order form. It looks tacky and cheapens the cookbook. But an individual or a community cookbook benefits by having an order form. It looks good and increases your sales. Whether you choose to include an order form or not is a matter of taste. Most of the cookbook printers offer this at no extra charge.

Pay careful attention to all the little details in every part of your cookbook. It makes a big difference. Consistency throughout your cookbook brings it together into a cohesive whole. The typestyle of the text on the front and back covers should be in harmony with the interior text; this will unify your cookbook.

Taking great care with writing your recipes and side items, styling and designing your pages, typesetting with easy-to-read, attractive fonts and pitch size, will cook up a cookbook you will be happy with, one you'll be proud to serve.

Writing a Back Cover Blurb

A back cover blurb—what your cookbook says about itself on the back cover—is one of the best selling tools for your cookbook. When people pick your cookbook off the shelf in a bookstore, either because the title appeals to them if it's shelved spine out, or because the front cover entices them, the very next thing they will do is read the back cover. A back cover blurb can be the deciding factor that either encourages someone to consider your cookbook and look through it or makes them put it back on the shelf.

A back cover blurb highlights the features of your cookbook and shows its benefits. Since you've written your cookbook, complete with story line and side items, sum it up on your back cover in a few clear, succinct paragraphs. Use bullets or culinary clip art to show the benefits. If you've obtained favorable endorsements from notable people and/or book reviewers, include one or two of the quotes on your back cover blurb.

Back covers have a fairly standard format. In the upper left corner is the genre. In your case, this will be Cooking. You can further clarify the category of your cookbook. If it is a diet or a health-related cookbook, show Cooking/Diet or Cooking/Health. In the upper right corner is the price. The price, along with the ISBN, will also be embedded in the bar code, which is placed at the bottom right. Put your publisher name, and logo if you have one, on the bottom left. If you have a website, show it directly under your publisher name.

Read the back cover blurbs on lots of cookbooks to see what they say and to determine what makes them appealing. Make your back cover blurb so appealing and enticing, so inviting and delicious, that the person reading it will just have to have your cookbook.

Since there's so much white space on this page, here's another recipe you might enjoy making or including in your cookbook:

Chunky Chicken Sandwich

I first enjoyed this sandwich at a restaurant in Wisconsin. It was so good that I asked the chef for the recipe. The combination of ingredients play together in your mouth like a symphony.

1 cup cooked chicken breast,
   coarsely chopped
1/2 cup seedless green or purple grapes,
   washed and quartered
1/4 cup coarsely chopped almonds
3 T. mayonnaise or salad dressing
4 Kaiser rolls or hamburger buns

Garnish –
1 stalk celery, julienned
1 carrot, julienned

In a medium-size mixing bowl, combine the chicken, grapes, and almonds together with the mayonnaise.

Chef's Tip: Julienne is a French term meaning to slice thinly into matchsticks, about 2 inches in length.

Presentation: Serve on buns with julienned celery and carrot sticks on the side.

Chapter Five

Breads & Rolls

Before you typeset your cookbook and go to press, proof your cookbook, then proof it again. When you make bread, you proof the dough, letting it rise, so proof your cookbook to make sure it's perfect, there are no errors, and you're completely happy with it.

Don't count on the spellchecker function on your computer to catch all your typos. It will catch the obvious ones but miss many important ones. For example, if you type tee instead of tea, the spellchecker will go right over it. Read your cookbook thoroughly, line by line. Now is also the time to put all your commas in the right place, make sure you didn't drop any ingredients, double-check that your abbreviations are consistent, and your directions are clear and user-friendly.

When you think your cookbook is the best it can be, make photocopies of it and ask your friends or some of the people in your group or organization to read and proof your cookbook and give you their feedback and opinions. Give them a red pencil and ask them to mark up your manuscript. Offer them a free meal for their help.

This will help you hone your cookbook to perfection, plus your readers can catch any stray typos or omissions. Sometimes we're so close to our work that we don't see the (often glaring) flaws in our writing. Once your cookbook is perfected and published, you'll roll in the dough (money).

Speaking of money, now is the time to get serious about pricing your cookbook. Look at cookbooks on the bookstore shelves which are similar to yours in content, design, binding, and number of recipes. See how much they cost to help you determine the right price for your cookbook. Price your cookbook competitively; price it to make a profit.

While you're setting the price, think about all the extras you'll need to promote your cookbook. Some of your advertising, such as press releases, book reviews, and word of mouth, will be free, but you'll have to come up with the dough for your printed promotional materials and food for your cooking demonstrations.

These will help get the word out about your cookbook. They'll be the bread and butter for on-going sales and promotion of your cookbook, and will help you raise more sales. Promotional materials will help your cookbook stand out from the crowd and be noticed.

Completing your cookbook, planning its promotion, and deciding what you'll need to launch it can be a stressful time. There are so many little and large details to attend to. You may be feeling a little burned out and more than a little stressed. If overwhelm or a case of overload hits you, you knead to relax, step back a bit and take a breather.

Every writer, no matter what they write, always steps back for a while to give themselves and their book a little space. Then they come back to it refreshed and with a clear eye and a sharp pencil, ready to finalize and fine-tune their book before sending it off to press or to their publisher.

You'd be amazed at how little errors will jump off the page, errors you overlooked the numerous times you read through your book. Even if you don't get overwhelmed, give yourself a break and take some time off from your cookbook. You'll both benefit from it.

This will also give you a good perspective and show you any changes that need to be made. This valuable time away from your cookbook will inspire even more ideas and give you clarity on the overall picture. Give yourself time to relax and clean up your cookbook before it goes to press.

You always proof bread twice and you'll be proofing your cookbook twice. A few weeks after you send it to the printer, or several months after you send it to your publisher, they will send you a proof of your cookbook, which is a replica of what your cookbook will look like when printed.

This typeset proof gives you another chance to make corrections if necessary. Changes at this point, unless they're the printer's or the publisher's mistakes, can be costly. Make sure your cookbook is perfect before you sent it to press.

While you're letting your cookbook rest before it goes to the printer, plan your promotions and make preliminary plans to put your promotions into action. Research your potential markets. Look into direct mail and premium sales. Contact local groups and businesses to set up cooking demonstrations when your cookbook is hot off the press.

Decide whether you'll store the cookbooks in a closet or in a warehouse, or if you'll use an order fulfillment service. The garage is not a good idea. Your cookbooks will mildew and smell musty. Who wants to buy a stinky cookbook? If you choose a warehouse, make sure it's climate controlled, the price is reasonable, and you have access to your cookbooks when you need them.

Now is the time to set up VISA and MasterCard merchant accounts, to obtain a toll-free number, to open a business checking account, to create a website, and to get a UPS or FedEx business account. Take care of the business aspects you'll need to have before your cookbook and promotional materials are printed.

Somewhere toward the end of writing your cookbook, make pre-pub announcements and offer advance sales to everyone you know, people you don't know, everyone in the community, and all the members in your group or organization. Send a colorful flyer, or place them in strategic locations, announcing that your cookbook is ready to go to press with the date you expect its return. Enclose an advance sale coupon or attach it to the flyer.

Print up advance sale coupons with the words $pecial $ale. Collect the cash up front. Offer a reduced price for pre-pub orders to make it enticing. Take $2.00 off the cover price. Coupons with your customer's name, address, and phone number make it easy to deliver the cookbooks after they're printed. Pre-pub sales also help you gauge the size of your print run.

Let the community know about your pre-pub sale by sending a press release to your local newspaper, describing your cookbook and giving a sample recipe from it. Be sure to include your contact information. Send your press release a month or two before you go to press. If the newspaper elects not to run your announcement, place an ad. Pre-pub sales often pay the printing bill before your cookbook is printed.

Consider selling advertising space in your cookbook if it is a community cookbook. Many local groups and businesses could benefit from advertising in your cookbook. Realtors, kitchen boutiques, restaurants, bakeries, retail stores, and food markets are just a few. Contact them and offer them the opportunity; tell them it will increase their visibility as well as their sales.

Determine the price you will charge them for their ads. Advertising space can be business card size all the way up to a full page. Offer your potential advertisers choices and promise them a freebie cookbook. These ads will be placed in the back matter of your cookbook after the index and before your order form.

Promotional Materials

When you're done proofing your cookbook, write your promotional materials while your cookbook is fresh in your mind. Think about the things that are special about your cookbook and highlight them in your promotional materials. Most of this information will be on the back cover blurb you wrote.

Be sure to include all the necessary information in all your promotional materials to make your cookbook available and accessible to the crowds of people who will want to buy it. Provide your bite and your contact information. Include all the important and pertinent data, such as ISBN, price, size of your cookbook, binding, number of pages, number of recipes, and shipping/handling charges. These are your book specs.

Your promotional materials will help get your cookbook noticed. Making your cookbook stand out from the crowd begins with a quality cookbook, one you're proud to serve. Your promotional materials and persistence in marketing will make your cookbook rise above the rest.

Your promotional materials include, but are not limited to: Colorful recipe cards, cookbook postcards, sell sheets/flyers, posters, refrigerator magnets, and overrun book covers. These will give your cookbook greater exposure and help raise more sales, interest a distributor in carrying your cookbook, and help you get your cookbook into bookstores, libraries, and plenty of other retail markets.

Target your promotional materials to your potential buyers. Put yourself in their place. Think in terms of what would appeal to them, what would make them want to buy your cookbook. Present your cookbook information in an enticing, inviting manner in all your promotional materials.

Have recipe cards printed with a recipe on the front. Put ordering information, a description of your cookbook—your bite—and book specs on the back. You'll need several sets of recipe cards with different recipes printed on each one. Choose your best recipes for your recipe cards.

Have postcards printed with your cookbook cover on the front. Place ordering information and other tidbits—your cookbook specs and bite—on the back, with space to address your postcards to your mailing list.

You'll need two different, yet similar, sets of flyers. One for distributors, wholesalers, bookstores, and other retail markets, and one for the general public to serve as one of your best advertising blurbs. These are also known as sell sheets. Design and print colorful flyers on 8-1/2 x 11-inch glossy paper showing the cookbook cover, bite, and book specs, with contact and ordering information.

For distributors, bookstores, and other retail markets, make your sell sheet businesslike; be sure to include your ISBN and price, pertinent information about your cookbook, and your discount schedule. For the general public, make your flyer more personal and show full price.

Maybe you'll want to plaster posters all over town, placing them in strategic locations where your target audience will see them. You can also use them when you do cooking demonstrations and book signings, and to advertise your presence in advance of a promotional event.

Refrigerator magnets are a great way to keep your cookbook in front of your buyers. They're so much better than a business card. Every time someone goes to their refrigerator, they will see your cookbook information. Many people stand in front of the fridge wondering what to make for dinner. Your cookbook magnet will offer them the answer.

Overrun book covers will be an important part of your marketing and promotion. Overrun book covers are copies of your front and back cover printed on the same stock your cookbook cover is printed on. Plan to order several hundred. You'll be sending them out with press releases, using them as advertising blurbs, and as selling tools to interest bookstore owners and retail stores in carrying your cookbook. Library and bookstore distributors require thirty to fifty overrun book covers for their sales reps on an initial order. If your cookbook sells well, they will request more.

Most printers can do these promotional materials when they print your cookbook, you can farm them out (see Appendix C), or have them done at your local print shop. Call around for prices. Ask for samples to see the quality of their work.

The day comes when you send your cookbook to the printer or your publisher. This is a special moment in your life. You've accomplished something very wonderful. You've written a cookbook and are about to become a published author. Celebrate this day to revel in your achievement. It's quite a high but after the glow wears off, you might feel let down and maybe even a bit sad.

You will also probably feel more than a little lost and not know what to do with yourself after you send your cookbook to press. You've spent so much time and energy, and devoted so much of your focus and attention into your cookbook, that you're bound to feel a little lost without it. Every writer experiences this.

Don't despair. You still have lots to do to prepare for your cookbook's return. Firm up and schedule your promotion and advertising plans. Write the ads (sell the sizzle) so they're ready to go when your cookbook is ready to go. You know your market and how to target and reach your buying audience.

Obtain targeted mailing lists if you plan to do a blitz mailing. A blitz mailing is huge, one that goes to everyone who is interested or who might be even remotely interested in buying your cookbook. Apply for bulk rate at the post office if your promotional mailing will be large enough to qualify for it. Type the mailing labels so your mailing will be ready to go when your cookbook arrives. Clarify and hone your list of reviewers that you'll send a review copy of your cookbook to. (See Appendix C and Appendix D.)

You'll find your hands full with everything you need to do. But don't bite off more than you can chew. Pace yourself. Prepare a plan of action, a to-do list, and do it. You'll be stepping up the momentum when you receive your cookbook.

Another important thing to do while your cookbook is baking at the printer is to write your press release. A press release gives all the appropriate and important information about your cookbook in a factual, journalistic format. You'll send your press release announcing the arrival of your cookbook to the media—newspapers, magazines, radio and TV stations—in a staggered timetable before your cookbook comes home.

Writing a press release is easy. In the top, right-hand corner, type **For Immediate Release**, or your intended release date (when you want the public to know about it) in big, bold letters. Place the date just under it. At the top left, type your contact information: Your name, organization name if applicable, phone number, and email.

Drop down a few spaces and center your cookbook title in big, bold letters. In lieu of that, or in addition to it, create a headline that will immediately attract the reader's attention and make them want to read more.

Type the body double-spaced in paragraph form. Write in the third person, as if someone else were writing about the cookbook and the author. Be sure to include your bite. Your press release should be short, clear, and to the point, providing only the important, necessary information in two or three paragraphs and omitting all the fluff. Think in terms of a newspaper article. Present the important information about your cookbook in a who, what, where, why, when, and how format.

Who wrote it, what it is—a cookbook with number of recipes, price, binding, and page count that offers such and such—where and when it will be available, why people will want to buy it, and how they can obtain it. Don't be surprised if a reporter from the newspaper contacts you and wants to do an interview. Jump at this opportunity for free publicity.

You might want to attach one or two of your best recipes and an overrun book cover. If you haven't received your overrun book covers from the printer, include a color photocopy of your cover (which the printer sent you with the proof). Jot a note at the bottom of your press release requesting that if there is room, a picture of the cover and a recipe or two be printed. (See the sample press release at the end of this chapter.)

Request to be placed in the food, cookbook review, what's new, lifestyle, or social section. You're more likely to reach your target audience, the people who are interested in cooking. Aim to have your press release printed in the weekend edition. It will be seen by more people. Send your press release to local newspapers, radio, and TV stations one month before your cookbook is due back from the printer or before your chosen pub date.

In addition to sending your press release to the local media, send it to hundreds of influential contacts. Think big; think national. You can obtain a press release mailing list in the *Gale Directory of Publications and Broadcast Media*. This directory lists the addresses and phone numbers of newspapers, radio, and television stations nationwide. This directory is available at the library or you can order a copy by calling 800/877-GALE, or by writing to Thomson-Gale Research, 27500 Drake Road, Farmington Hills, MI 48331-3535. It's rather expensive, so your best bet is to look through this 8-volume set at the library to select the media that best suits your cookbook.

On a national scope, send your press release six months in advance of your pub date. You might want to also include an overrun book cover, a recipe card, and/or a flyer with your book specs in this mailing. In your press release, state that review copies are available upon request. (We'll cover review copies in more detail in the next chapter.)

If your cookbook has regional interest, such as recipes and stories specific to your area, send your press release two months in advance of your pub date, along with a few sample recipes and an over-run book cover, to local and regional magazines.

Don't forget the biggies. You want as many people as possible to know about your cookbook. Send your press release and accompanying materials to food magazines and women's magazines, such as *Bon Appetit, Cooking Light, Woman's Day, Better Homes and Gardens, Redbook,* and *Good Housekeeping,* to name a few.

If your cookbook is a community cookbook and/or a fundraiser, send your press release to all the local associations and fraternal organizations that will be receptive to it. Inquire if they'll include information about your cookbook in their newsletter. Also contact your local chamber of commerce for a list of local newsletters to broaden the scope of your coverage.

Publishing a cookbook is exciting, and it's exciting news. You want to let the world know that your cookbook is about to be born. Being a cookbook author also makes you an exciting person to all the people who will want to interview you on radio and TV, for a newspaper article, and who will invite you to speak or do cooking demonstrations for their groups. You'll be in great demand; your cookbook will be your ticket. Your sales will soar and you'll roll in the dough.

The sample press release on the following page is a guide for you to use in writing a sizzling press release for your cookbook that will get you inundated with free press and requests for interviews.

Sample Press Release

Judy Matthews   **For Immediate Release**
Phone Number / email   Intended Release Date

Holy Smokes! Something's Burning!
Firehouse Fare and Food for Thought from Firefighters

A smokin' hot cookbook, just as important to have in your kitchen as a fire extinguisher, has been published by Judy Matthews. Mother of a firefighter, she took a citizens firefighting course—a hands-on, twelve-week composite of what firefighters learn in six months at the Fire Academy.

This $15.00 cookbook shows bite-size pieces of what was taught in class and experienced on ride-alongs for fire and ambulance calls, giving readers a look into a day in the life of a firefighter. Between calls, and hanging out at the fire station close to the stove to see what was cooking, Matthews interviewed hundreds of firefighters.

Holy Smokes offers 350 recipes from firefighters that are cooked at the stations. This softcover, comb-bound, 412-page cookbook includes home fire safety and fire prevention tips as well as first-hand experiences of firefighters.

Profits go to raise funds for fallen firefighters and their families. The cookbook is available at all local fire stations, grocery stores, and by calling 800/000-FIRE. Get your copies while they're hot!

# # #

Thank you for your attention to this. Attached is a cookbook cover and a recipe. If space is available, please print them with the press release. Review copies are available upon request.

Chapter Six

Desserts

Now that your cookbook is published and has come home, you deserve to enjoy your just desserts. You've written and published a cookbook and now it's time to party, to let the world, or at least your community, know that your cookbook is here. Celebrate with a launch party to show off your cookbook and get the sales in motion.

Launch your cookbook at a shopping mall or some other place where the public congregates. Have a huge kick-off party to start the sales. Invite everyone you know and tell them to invite everyone they know. Be sure to invite the media; you want to get the launch party in the news. Also invite the mayor and elected officials, all the store owners in town who may want to offer your cookbook for sale in their stores, and everyone else you can think of.

Judy Matthews launched *Holy Smokes* at an open house at a fire station. The entire community was invited. There was a lot of advance advertising and press coverage. Several local restaurants donated food. Fire safety pamphlets were handed out, children were given plastic fire hats and small rubber fire engines, adults got refrigerator magnets, there were drawings for free T-shirts, and everyone got an informative tour of the station. More than 2,000 copies were sold in one day.

If your budget doesn't allow for a big party, get permission from the store manager and launch your cookbook in a grocery store on a crowded Saturday. Set up a table with an attractive display of your cookbook and food samples near the entrance so you can greet people, offer them a taste of your recipes, and show them your cookbook.

If you don't catch them on the way in, talk to them as they walk out the door with their grocery cart full of food. Mention that your cookbook will help them create delicious meals with the food they've bought. Suggest a recipe or two that they might like to prepare. Give them a recipe card. Be aggressive and polite.

Get together with your friends, or with the people in your group or organization, to cook up ideas for your launch party. Make your launch party unique. It's your cookbook and you can launch it anywhere and any way that you desire.

Launching your cookbook to the community is just the beginning. You'll want to announce your cookbook to the world through the press release you wrote in the previous chapter, by sending your cookbook for reviews, and by getting lots of media attention for free publicity.

In addition to the press release you'll send to local newspapers announcing the publication of your cookbook, send a press kit to key newspapers and food magazines that will be interested in reviewing your cookbook and possibly writing an article or doing an interview.

A press kit is enclosed in a 9 x 12 pocket folder. Place your cookbook in the right side pocket. Your cover letter, press clippings—if your cookbook has already been reviewed or if an article has been printed—rave endorsements from chefs, recipe cards, sell sheets/flyers, press releases, copies of published recipes, an overrun book cover, and other items of this nature go in the left side pocket. Decorate the outside of the folder with a postcard of your cookbook cover glued to the front.

Book reviews are a vital, important part of selling your cookbook. There are two different ways to obtain book reviews, depending on how many cookbooks you've set aside as review copies. Either send a cover letter with a copy of your cookbook and other promotional materials (press kit), or send a cover letter, along with an overrun book cover and a few sample recipes, to the food editor at key newspapers and magazines, and to people in the media and book reviewers to see if they'd be interested in reviewing your cookbook. When they respond with interest, send them a copy of your cookbook. This is called a review copy.

Be generous in sending review copies to people in the media and book reviewers, but also be aware that a few people will request a copy of your cookbook without the slightest intention of reviewing it. Cookbooks are enormously popular items. (See Appendix D for a list of book reviewers.)

Begin your media blitz. Use free advertising and publicity to your advantage. Send the press release you wrote announcing your cookbook to local newspapers, radio and TV stations. If your cookbook is a community cookbook, get your launch party listed on the schedule of community events in the newspaper and on your local radio and TV stations.

A community calendar announces events that are open and free to the public. When you hold an event, such as your launch party, book signings, and cooking demonstrations, local radio and TV stations will announce it on their community calendars. To request that your event be announced, send a press release about your event a month in advance to the station's community affairs director.

If you are raising funds for a charitable cause, a public service announcement (PSA) is another way to let people in your community know about your cookbook and the cause it supports. Contact local radio and TV stations to provide them with information about your cookbook and your cause.

Your cookbook is news. To get on the news—to let the greatest number of people know about your cookbook—contact the program director at local TV stations and suggest an interview. If they have a cooking segment, tell them you'd love to come in to talk about your cookbook and do a cooking demonstration.

Let your voice be heard. To get on the radio, follow the same procedure. Contact the program director at local radio stations that will be interested in talking to you on the air about your cookbook.

This may take some doing. People are very busy at TV and radio stations, and are overwhelmed with ideas suggested by the public. Start with a letter and enclose an overrun book cover, along with a few recipe cards. Your letter may get lost in the shuffle. If there is no response within two weeks, follow up with a phone call. Be persistent, pleasant, and positive. Come up with creative ways to get their attention. You've written a cookbook, so you might want to send some non-perishable food you've made. That will definitely get noticed, but it may also look like a bribe. Use your best judgment.

Give interviews to all the newspaper reporters, disc jockeys, and TV people who contact you. Tell them about the plans for your launch party. Give reporters a copy of your cookbook or an overrun book cover; ask them to include a photo of it and information on how to buy your cookbook in their article. You'll get loads of orders.

Announce the launch party on the air when you do radio interviews. Invite all the listeners to attend; give time, date, and location. Flash your cookbook on TV, tell all the viewers where they can buy it, and invite them to your launch party.

In addition to your press release announcing the publication of your cookbook, send a letter and another press release announcing your launch party to the food editor at your local newspaper. Enclose a few recipe cards, along with an overrun book cover or a cookbook postcard. Ask for three things: That the title of your cookbook be mentioned with the recipes; that the cookbook cover be shown if space allows; and that information be given on your launch party.

Place posters all over town with information on your launch party. Be sure to put lots of posters in and around the place where you will be having your launch party. Place ads in the local newspaper announcing your launch party before, during, and after your interview is printed in the paper, you appear on TV, and you are heard on the radio. If there is a community newsletter in your area, place an ad there, too, inviting everyone to come to your launch party.

Timing and saturation are important. People will read the article, listen to you on the radio, watch you on TV, see the ads and colorful posters you've plastered all over town, and notice your recipes in the newspaper. They'll begin to think your cookbook is a big deal and that they just have to have a copy. They'll be sure to attend your launch party. If they don't show up at your party, they'll probably walk into a bookstore to buy a copy of your cookbook.

After your interviews and media appearances, and before the article comes out, the TV and radio shows air, contact bookstores in your area. Tell the managers about the article and when it's due to be printed, when the TV show will air, and when the radio show will be heard. Ask them to stock your cookbook so it will be available at their store for all the hungry people who are going to rush right in and buy it.

Better yet, contact them before you do newspaper, radio, and TV interviews. Ask them to stock your cookbook. Offer them the standard bookstore discount of 40% off the cover price. Tell them you'll announce to the reading, listening, and viewing audiences that your cookbook is available at their store. They'll love the traffic you'll pull in.

Tell the same bookstore managers who will stock your cookbook that you'd be happy to come in and do a book signing. A huge book signing at a big bookstore could also be your launch party. Create a festive atmosphere by decorating with balloons and streamers for a birthday party theme. It's your cookbook's birthday and that's cause for celebration. Make several cake recipes from your cookbook to serve.

If you've published a fundraising cookbook, approach bakeries and grocery stores to donate the cakes. Many local businesses are happy to support your cause. It creates goodwill in the community, draws attention and free advertising to their business, and reflects a positive image for them. Don't be shy about contacting them and asking for what you want or need.

At your book signing/birthday party, don't sit behind the table of your cookbooks and cake waiting for people to come to you, even though most will because of the free food. Have one or two friends, or a few people from your group, sit at the table while you wander around the store with your cookbook in hand. Offer cake to all the customers and give them a recipe card of your cake recipe or tell them who donated the cake. Show them your cookbook, tell them about its many delicious features, and invite them over to your table for cake and a copy of your cookbook, which you'll be pleased to autograph. Even if they don't want to buy your cookbook, graciously give them cake anyway.

In addition to arranging book signings in bookstores, visit all the retail locations in town, with your cookbook and sell sheet, where you think they will be interested in offering your cookbook. Talk to the manager and arrange a book signing, with or without a cooking demonstration, or ask the manager to place your cookbook for sale in the store.

There are so many more things you can do to sell your cookbook. Press releases, promotional materials, a launch party, newspaper ads, on-air interviews, book reviews, press kits, cooking demonstrations, and book signings are just the beginning. There are hundreds of ways to market and promote your cookbook. Chapter Eight lists 101 ways to make super sales.

If you'd like to, and you have the bucks in your budget, hire a publicist to write and send out your press releases, to create ads, to arrange tours and book signings, and to set up interviews with the press and on radio and TV. A publicist has media connections and can help get the word out about your cookbook.

You can do everything a publicist can do and it's probably more fun to market and promote your cookbook yourself. You wrote it, created and developed the recipes, and devoted a huge chunk of your time and energy. You know best how to promote it and where to sell it. If you do hire a publicist, you'll have to feed him or her your unique marketing ideas, along with cold cash.

In addition to marketing and promoting your cookbook, take some time to taste the sweet success of the fruits of your labors. Enter your cookbook in contests to win awards. This is icing on the cake. Award-winning cookbooks will get you even more media attention and garner greater sales. (See Appendix B.)

Connect your cookbook with a corporation for premium sales. Cookbooks are a natural in this area. Show off your cookbook on websites and in cookbook catalogs to provide wider coverage for your promotion dollars. (See Appendix C.)

After all this hoopla—launching your cookbook and getting the word out about it—you deserve a rest. Take some time just for you and indulge yourself with a sweet treat.

Chapter Seven

Cookies & Candy

Make your cookbook available to everyone who wants to buy it. There are lots of ways to achieve this. Bookstores are probably your first thought. Beyond bookstores, there are many other avenues to pursue that will get your cookbook into libraries, gift shops, retail stores, grocery stores, bakeries, and kitchen boutiques, to name a few. The next chapter lists numerous ways to pursue alternate markets.

Placing your cookbook in major bookstores can be a bit difficult without a distributor because the major chains—Borders and Barnes & Noble—are rather picky about buying self-published books from the authors. There's a way around this. Start little and local.

Independent, privately-owned bookstores are more willing to take your cookbook on consignment. Consignment means they'll offer your cookbook for sale in the store, pay after the books are sold, and return them if they're not sold, usually within ninety days.

Get up close and personal. Call the manager of every bookstore, gift shop, kitchen boutique, bakery, grocery store, deli, and retail store in your area where you think your cookbook will be appropriate. Set up an appointment to meet with him or her. Bring a sell sheet, some promotional materials, and a copy of your cookbook to show. Tell the manager about your cookbook, stressing that it will sell well in the store because of your promotional efforts, and that it will also increase profits for the business. Offer the standard 40% discount. Be charming and pleasantly aggressive. Make them an offer they can't refuse.

Keep a box of books in your car. When the manager says, "Yes, we'll take ten copies on consignment," run out to your car and get them. Obtain a receipt for the books and give the manager an invoice which you'll fill in with the appropriate number of books and the discount agreed upon.

Offer to autograph your cookbooks. Autographed copies sell much better and cannot be returned. Another way to increase visibility and local sales for your cookbook is to autograph any remaining in-store copies after a book signing. Talk to the bookstore manager and tell him/her you'd be happy to autograph copies of your cookbook. They will put a sticker on your cookbook which says Autographed Copy. The bookstore employees will often hand-sell your cookbook because they've met you—the cookbook author.

If some of the bookstores and other retail markets where you want to place your cookbook are a bit further out of your area, do telemarketing. I did this with my first self-published book and sold 300 copies the first week. Call and introduce yourself, or your group or organization. Tell the manager about your cookbook and its best selling features. Ask if the store would be interested in offering it for sale on consignment. Be enthusiastic and positive. Put a big smile on your face when you're on the phone. The person you're speaking with can't see your smile but will hear it in your voice.

Telemarketing works wonderfully well with stores in your area because you're a local author. If they don't seem interested at first, say that you'd like to send them some information about your cookbook. Follow up right away so your communication will be fresh in their mind when they receive your materials. Write a nice letter reiterating your telephone conversation. Enclose your sell sheet, an overrun book cover, a refrigerator magnet, and a few recipe cards.

Some stores that you contact by phone, and even ones you visit in person, will request a review copy—a freebie—saying that they have to see the book first before they'll agree to sell it in their store, or that they don't have time to look at it right now, but if you leave a copy, they'll look it over and get back to you. Both sound like a reasonable request on the surface, but be a little wary about this. Keep in mind that most books are ordered sight unseen.

Bookstores and other retail markets can be rather unscrupulous about this—keeping your review copy and selling it, not bothering to pay you for it, and not ordering any books in the future. If a store requests a review copy, go with your feelings about it. If they seem really interested in your cookbook and think it will sell well in their store, give them a review copy. If it seems they're not very interested, but request a free copy of your cookbook, offer a sell sheet and an overrun book cover first. Remind them that you're offering your cookbook on consignment, which means no risk to them.

When you provide review copies of your cookbook, write or stamp Review Copy or attach a mailing label inside the front cover with the words Review Copy. Include your contact and ordering information. Books that are marked in this way cannot be sold.

When bookstores take books on consignment, they pay after they sell your books, usually within 90 to 120 days. They require a 40% discount, plus you pay shipping. If you're visiting the stores in person, take your cookbooks with you. If, after a certain amount of time, the store has not been able to sell your cookbooks, they will return them to you. You also have to pay the freight to get them back. If it's a local store, you can go in and get them.

Mailing through the post office can become quite expensive and the post office is notorious for losing mail. It might be a good idea to set up a UPS account to ship all the cookbooks you will be sending out. There are two types of UPS accounts. One is a pick-up account where they pick up from you on a daily or a weekly basis; the other is a lugger account where you lug your cookbooks to the UPS facility. Determine which account will be right for you. Pick-up is more expensive; lugger is more legwork.

In lieu of a UPS account, you might want to use an order fulfillment service. If you think you can sell hundreds or thousands of cookbooks, this will save you a lot of time and energy, not to mention the drudgery of packaging and shipping your cookbooks, typing invoices, and trying to collect payment from customers.

An order fulfillment service will warehouse your cookbooks, provide a toll-free number for you to give to your customers, accept payment, ship your cookbooks out, and pay you. There is a per book fee for this service as well as a set-up fee and an inventory maintenance fee, which is a charge to store your books.

Speaking of shipping, you'll need boxes and padded mailing envelopes to ship your cookbooks in. Your local office supply store has these. A less expensive outlet is Quill Office Supplies, a mail-order house. Call 800/789-1331 to request a catalog and to set up an account with them or visit their website at www.quill.com. They have all the quality supplies you need at a discounted price and offer free shipping on orders over $45.00.

While we're on the subject of office supplies, you'll also need #10 business envelopes and mailing labels with your publisher name and address. Business cards are a good thing to have to enclose with your cookbooks and correspondence. If you don't plan to generate computer-printed invoices, you might want pre-printed invoices. Your local print shop can help you with these or you can order through Quill, which also offers printing services.

We got a little sidetracked here. Let's go back to the stores. When you're selling your cookbook in person or over the phone, entice the managers of bookstores and retail shops by offering them a special introductory price of 50% off the cover price. Offer free shipping if they're too far for you to travel to bring the cookbooks in.

When you send the books, or bring them in, enclose an invoice with the date, your invoice number, cookbook title, ISBN, quantity of books, discount, shipping charges if applicable, and payment terms. You'll probably have to settle for consignment but try for net 30 days. If the store has given you a purchase order number, include that on your invoice.

Borders has a Community Relations Consultant (CRC) in almost every bookstore. Call and make an appointment. Show up with your sell sheet and a copy of your cookbook in hand. Tell the CRC that you're a local author and they will take ten copies of your cookbook on consignment for their store only.

To get into Borders all over the country, send two review copies of your cookbook, along with a cover letter, marketing plan, and proposed terms to New Vendor Acquisitions, Borders Group, Inc., 100 Phoenix Drive, Ann Arbor, MI 48108. Phone: 734/477-1100. www.borders.com. Getting your cookbook accepted into Borders will also get it placed in Waldenbooks.

Barnes & Noble won't take copies on consignment, no matter how nice you are or how much you beg. They'll tell you to contact their corporate office in New York and give you a form, with contact information, to fill out and send in with your cookbook and marketing plan. You can get this same information on their website at www.bn.com. Send a cover letter and one review copy to Marcella Smith, Barnes & Noble, Small Press Department, 122 Fifth Avenue, New York, NY 10011. Phone: 212/633-3454. They will usually order a small quantity of five cookbooks and will place them in your local Barnes & Noble. If they sell, they will order more copies, usually through your distributor.

Don't forget Books-A-Million. Even though they don't have stores in all the states, they are a major bookstore chain. Send a cover letter and one review copy to New Acquisitions, American Wholesale Book Company, 131 South 25th Street, Irondale, AL 35210. Phone: 205/956-4151. Call the Publisher Information Hotline at 205/956-4151, ext. 300 to get more information about what to send and how to send it or visit their website at www.booksamillion.com.

Little and local is easy. Regional and national can be a bit of a challenge. If you want the corporate book buyers at the major chains to select your cookbook, approach them professionally. Provide all the information requested and send a review copy of your cookbook in your press kit. The buyers will want to know how you plan to promote your cookbook to drive customers into their store to buy it. Your marketing plan is critical and crucial information.

If they think you will promote your cookbook in a big way, and that you have lots of energy and enthusiasm to do so, they might try your cookbook in several of their key stores, along with placing one or two copies of your cookbook in your local store. If your cookbooks sell well, they will direct you to a distributor, if you don't already have one, usually Baker & Taylor, and order in quantity from them.

Speaking of Baker & Taylor, they also distribute to libraries. Contact them at 1120 Route 22 East, Bridgewater, NJ 08807, call them at 800/775-1500, or visit their website at www.btol.com. Direct your inquiries to Publisher's Services. Almost all bookstores order from Baker & Taylor.

Another major bookstore distributor is Ingram Book Company. Contact the Book Buyer at One Ingram Boulevard, La Vergne, TN 37086, call them at 800/937-8222 or visit their website at www.ingrambook.com. Email: bookbuyer@ingrambook.com.

Both Baker & Taylor and Ingram are wholesalers rather than distributors. This means they don't have sales reps to sell your cookbook to bookstores and libraries. They send you a purchase order and ship your cookbooks when they are ordered. They charge a database fee but having a distributor is worth the price because you won't be able to get your cookbook into most bookstores and libraries without going through normal distribution channels.

Your local library will buy a copy of your cookbook simply because you're a local author. To get your cookbook into thousands of libraries, you'll need a library distributor. Quality Books and Unique Books both distribute exclusively to libraries and it is fairly easy to get them to represent your cookbook, provided that you have a quality cookbook and the binding is appropriate.

Contact Quality Books at 1003 West Pines Road, Oregon, IL 61061, Attn: New Title Acquisitions. Call them at 815/732-4450 to inquire about their procedure for accepting books or visit their website at www.qualitybooks.com.

Ditto for Unique Books. They are located at 5010 Kemper Avenue, St. Louis, MO 63139. Call them at 800/533-5446 and request a vendor information packet. Their website is exclusively for library use.

The nice thing about selling your cookbook to libraries, even though they usually buy only one copy, is that once you sell them your cookbook, your cookbook is sold. Libraries don't return books. They keep them. People who check out your cookbook from a library may want to buy a copy for themselves. This is where your order form, your 800 number if you have one, your website, and your VISA/MasterCard status will come in handy.

Another way to get your cookbook into libraries is by getting rave reviews. Libraries buy books based on book reviews, as well as through sales reps. (See Appendix D for a list of book reviewers.) When the library notices the reviews, the book buyer for the library will order the book through Baker & Taylor or another wholesaler.

Another innovative way to sell your cookbook to libraries is to have your friends and family all over the country go into their local library and ask for your cookbook. When a library gets two or three requests for the same book in a short amount of time, they usually decide to order it for their patrons. This is also a great technique to use for bookstores, although they will most likely offer to order only one copy for the customer who requests it.

Speaking of cross-country marketing, ask your friends and family who live in different states to personally contact all the bookstores and retail shops in their area. Provide them with your business cards and promotional materials—sell sheets, overrun book covers, recipe cards, refrigerator magnets—and lots of copies of your cookbook to show and sell.

Doing the distribution route is the best way to get your book into numerous bookstores and libraries. They prefer to order your cookbook from a distributor, rather than from you. It's just too much paperwork and a big hassle to order from a large number of self-publishers. They like one-stop shopping.

You can have more than one distributor or wholesaler. Just make sure you don't sign an exclusive contract or distribution agreement with them. Look in *Literary Market Place*, available at your local library, to find a distributor(s). (Also see Appendix D for cookbook-specific distributors.) Once you've found a few likely candidates, call to request the procedure for submitting your cookbook for representation.

Getting a distributor can be a bit difficult because they tend to want publishers with a line of books and a big promotion budget to push them; they look down on publishers who have only one or two books on their list. Getting a wholesaler is a whole lot easier. While you're looking for distributors to represent your cookbook, you'll come across many listings for wholesalers. The terms are somewhat interchangeable, though there's a big difference between wholesalers and distributors, as well as some similarities.

Distributors have their own sales force who go into the book-stores to sell your book, to get you shelf space. They will stock your books in their warehouse. Wholesalers don't actively sell your book or stock it. They rely on individual orders generated from bookstores and libraries. When an order for your cookbook is received by them, they will send you a purchase order for the number of copies they need from you, the vendor.

Distributors and wholesalers require you to sign a contract, pay a database fee—anywhere from $125.00 to $500.00—which will get your cookbook into their system, give them a 55% discount, and pay the shipping (freight) on books you send them. They usually pay 90 days after invoice but are notoriously slow when sending checks to you.

The Internet offers several large online bookstores: www.amazon. com, www.bn.com, www.booksamillion.com, and www.borders.com. They will show your cookbook with the cover graphic and in some cases, allow you to insert excerpts (recipes), author comment, publisher comment, table of contents, back cover blurb, and author bio. If you have a website and are not set up to col-lect money, link your website to theirs so that everyone who visits your website will be directed to theirs to buy your cookbook.

By the way, you don't need to do anything to get your cookbook listed on these websites. They will pick up your cookbook specs from the pre-pub data you supplied in your ABI form to *Books in Print* and *Forthcoming Books*. If you'd like to supply graphics and content material about your cookbook, visit their websites for their procedures about submitting additional information.

Don't overlook these online bookstores: www.betterworld.com, www.alibris.com, www.biggerbooks.com, www.overstock.com. www.powells.com, www.target.com, www.abebooks.com, and www.BookRun.com.

There are several online bookstores that are exclusively for cookbooks. Check out these websites to list your cookbook: www.ecookbooks.com, www.foodbooks.com, www.cookbookstore. com, and www.cookbookswelove.com.

Wholesalers and online bookstores will send you a STOP order when a customer orders your cookbook. A STOP order doesn't mean stop; it means Single Title Order Plan. Once in a while you will get a SCOP—Single Copy Order Plan. You send your cookbook and in 90 days or so, they will pay you.

Online bookstores require a 40% discount (sometimes more, if they've discounted your book to their customers) and will occasionally prepay the order and pay for shipping if you request it. Individual (STOP) orders from bookstores, where a customer walks in to the store and orders your book if it isn't on the shelf, are a pretty nice deal. The bookstore wants a 40% discount but will pay shipping charges, usually $4.00. They will also prepay the order if you request it. If not, you'll have to send an invoice when you ship the cookbook and pray they will pay you.

It's nice when the checks start rolling in, but beware! Some bookstores and other retail shops who have ordered your cookbook will somehow forget to pay you, even after you call, email, visit them if they're local, send duplicate invoices, and request the money that is rightfully yours. That's just the way the cookie crumbles. Rip-offs happen. When they do, just shrug your shoulders and let it go. It's never pleasant, but you can take these losses as a business deduction.

One way to minimize your risk is to give only one or two cookbooks on consignment, with the stipulation that after the consignment copies sell, the bookstore will put you on an individual ordering schedule, with the normal 40% discount and net 30 days payment or will order cookbooks from your distributor or wholesaler. You might want to offer them a 45% discount if the order is prepaid.

Another thing to be aware of is that bookstores and retail outlets have the right to return your cookbook if it doesn't sell, even though they've ordered it from you or your distributor. Returns are a standard policy, one that is rather unique to the book industry. They'll keep your cookbook on the shelf for anywhere from a few weeks to a few months. Some pay the freight back; most don't.

If your cookbooks are returned, they usually look shopworn. Their covers may be scuffed or bent, there might be spilled coffee on them, there could be torn pages, and your cookbook may have been stickered with a store barcode and price that is nearly impossible to remove. If you do manage to get it off, there will be a permanent sticky spot where the sticker was. These books are known as hurt books because they cannot be sold. You don't have to trash them; recycle them into review copies.

When all is said and done, it's a very special, wonderful thing to walk into a bookstore and see your cookbook on the shelf. Visit the bookstores in your area that stock your cookbook. Go into the cookbook section, find your cookbook, and place it face out at eye level where people will be sure to notice it. I learned this little trick from one of my publishers.

Chapter Eight

This & That

At the end of every cookbook there is usually a section for stuff like sauces, seasonings, dressings, and gravies that don't fit anywhere else in your cookbook. You'll find all the ingredients—the sauces, seasonings, and dressings—for super ways to make super sales of your cookbook here. Sauces, seasonings, and dressings do more than make your meal delicious; they can make or break your cookbook. Getting on the gravy train covers the extra sales of your cookbook beyond bookstores and libraries.

In addition to the ideas presented in earlier chapters and the 101 ways to market your cookbook listed here, look through the books in the recommended reading list on marketing and promotion (Appendix E) to gather even more ideas.

1. Count on your friends, family, neighbors, and co-workers for your first sales. They'll buy several copies to give to their friends, family, neighbors, and co-workers. Your family and friends will buy lots of copies to show your cookbook off to everyone they know.

2. The people who collaborated on your cookbook and contributed recipes are a built-in market. You can count on each person to buy two or three copies, maybe more. Name names, either under the recipe they've provided or mention them on your Acknowledgments page. People love to see their name in print.

3. If a chef or two has contributed recipes to your cookbook, they'll buy copies for their friends and family. Additionally, the restaurant where they work will often buy copies for sale to their customers, showing off the chef's featured recipes.

4. This also works well for local celebrities. Ask them to contribute a recipe or two for your cookbook. Approach the mayor, the

TV news people, and other influential people in your area. This can pay off in big dividends, not only because your cookbook will sell more copies with celebrity recipes, but because the local media are involved and may be willing to help promote your cookbook.

5. Sell your cookbook to the students in your cooking classes. They'll love to buy a copy with all its great recipes because they know you're a wonderful cook.

6. If you don't teach cooking classes, contact cooking instructors in your area. Ask if they'll feature some of your recipes in their classes and offer your cookbook for sale to their students. Tell them you'd be happy to come in and demonstrate a few of your recipes.

7. When this works, and it will, broaden your horizons. Contact instructors at cooking schools around the country. Mention your local success and offer to let them use and sell your cookbook in their classes. Give them the standard bookstore discount.

8. Offer yourself as a rent-a-chef; include your cookbook as part of your fee. Since you're an expert in cooking—you published a cookbook, didn't you?—people will be clamoring for you to come into their homes and cook delicious dinners for them. You'll earn a nice fee and they'll recommend you and your cookbook to everyone they know.

9. Create a catering business, using recipes from your cookbook. Cook for brunches, luncheons, and social events; serve your cookbook on the side.

10. After you've written, published, and promoted your cookbook, offer your services as a cookbook consultant to other people who want to write a cookbook. Your clients will want a copy of your cookbook, included in your fee, to see the great job you've done and to gather ideas and inspiration from you.

11. Show off your cookbook and your cooking. Give cooking demonstrations and offer taste samples. Any place that has kitchen facilities such as Whole Foods, which has a classroom with a built-in kitchen, is a great place to demonstrate your recipes and sell your cookbook.

Free food always appeals to people. Show them how to cook several recipes from your cookbook and give them a taste, along with recipe cards of what they're sampling. They'll want more than a few recipe cards, though, once they taste your food. They'll want your cookbook.

This works extremely well. Sampling sells. At Book Expo, commercial publishers of cookbooks sponsor a Cookbook Expo. A kitchen is built in part of the exhibition hall, local culinary arts students come in and cook the food, the chef gives a talk, the booksellers are fed a fabulous feast—using several recipes from the cookbook—and the chef-author autographs free copies of the cookbook. The booksellers practically trip over each other to place orders for cookbooks to sell in their stores.

12. Be a guest speaker at groups and organizations in your area. Talk about food; gear your speech to their needs. Show them how to cook easy, nutritious meals to fit their busy lifestyles. Have your cookbook there for sale to the members. This is known as back-of-the-room sales. Some groups will pay you a speaker's fee; this is a nice bonus.

13. If your cookbook is geared for a specialty, or niche, market, pursue that market. Say you've written a hardcover, fully illustrated cookbook of wok recipes. Contact higher-end stores that carry woks, such as Bed, Bath and Beyond, Linens 'n Things—they both have a huge kitchen section—and World Market. Ask them to place your cookbook next to the woks or suggest that they include it as part of a package deal: Buy a wok and get the cookbook with it. This is called bundling.

Here are a few more examples of niche marketing: *The Florida Citrus Cookbook* is sold at citrus stands across that state. *The California Seafood Book* is sold at hundreds of fish markets. *Tee Time at the Masters* sells tremendously well at golf courses, in sporting goods departments—placed next to the golf clubs—and at hotels with golf courses. Get the idea? Market your cookbook in all the niches it will fit into.

14. Sponsor a food trivia contest in the newspaper with your cookbook being the prize. This serves several good purposes. You'll get free advertising for your cookbook. After the prize-winning entry, all the remaining entries will provide you with a mailing list of

people who are interested in food and cooking. Send them a flyer and a letter, thanking them for their entry. Enclose a refrigerator magnet and offer $2.00 or $3.00 off your cookbook for entering the contest.

15. Go to Bingo Night and give your cookbook as the prize. Make a big fan-fare about presenting the winner with it. Bring boxes of your cookbook because lots of people there will want to buy it.

16. Attend a pot-luck dinner at a church, school, or other organization in your community. Make your best recipe to share and have lots of cookbooks for sale. Give everyone a recipe card of the dish you've made.

17. If you haven't submitted recipes to the food section of your local newspaper, now is the time to start while you're writing your cookbook. Send in a few of your best recipes that will be featured in your cookbook. Mention in your cover letter that you're writing a cookbook and when it will be available. Follow-up with your press release and a few more recipes when your cookbook is published.

18. Food co-ops are a great place to sell your cookbook because food is involved. Many schools offer food co-ops with a once-a-month market day designed to raise funds for school projects. Talk to the principal of the school and the co-op manager. Offer them $2.00 or $3.00 from the sale of every cookbook for their fundraising projects. More than likely, they'll be happy to set you up at a table to sell your cookbook. They may even include a brief blurb about your cookbook on the order form which is sent to parents and participants each month.

19. Local food pantries and food banks supply food to needy people in your community. Offer to let them sell your cookbook to the residents of the community to help support the food bank. Give them a generous discount, with the proceeds from the sale of your cookbook going to the food pantry. There's an extra bonus in this for you. This is one of those things that make you feel good, plus you're helping to feed people who are hungry.

Make it easy for residents to buy your cookbook. Sometimes local grocery stores support and/or sponsor the food bank. Ask them to make your cookbook available in their stores. The food bank will probably write an article about your cookbook in the community newsletter, giving you more publicity for your cookbook and inspiring more people to contribute to the food bank by buying your cookbook.

20. Farmer's markets are a bonanza for cookbook sales. Rent booth space at these outdoor markets throughout the summer to sell your cookbook. Offer samples or sell food made from your recipes, along with your cookbook. Food may not be an option, however. Many promoters of these markets require that you have insurance to sell or sample food.

21. Flea markets are another great place to sell your cookbook. Many flea markets are open, indoor and outdoor, year-round. They won't let you serve food because of health and insurance reasons, and because they usually have a food concession to feed the crowds. You'll have to reduce the price of your cookbook because people who go to flea markets expect a bargain.

22. The individual proprietors and businesses who bought advertising space in your cookbook—if you've done this—will buy copies to give to their friends and family, and very likely will offer it for sale to their clients or customers through their mailing list or in their place of business.

23. When you deliver your advertiser's complimentary copy, bring along a few cookbooks to offer for consignment. Help them arrange a visually-appealing display for your cookbook. If they have a store front, ask if you can create a decorative window display featuring your cookbook.

Even if local businesses have not bought advertising space in your cookbook, visit them with a copy of your cookbook and sell sheet. Ask if they will sell it in their place of business. Placing your cookbook in unlikely places will make it stand out and be noticed. Offer to create an attractive display showcasing your cookbook.

If their business lends itself to it, and even if it doesn't, suggest doing a cooking demonstration. If that's not do-able, offer to bring samples of prepared food. Walk around their business or store offering samples to all the clients or customers. While you're feeding them, give them a recipe card and show them your cookbook. Tell them you'd be happy to autograph their copy.

24. Take lots of copies of your cookbook to tailgate parties. There's always plenty of camaraderie there. When other people see and smell the food you're cooking, they'll wander over and strike up a conversation. Offer them a taste, tell them you wrote a cookbook and show it to them. This will draw a crowd and you'll sell lots of cookbooks.

25. Send cookbook postcards to everyone you know, people you barely know, and people you don't know at all. It's less expensive than mailing a flyer, plus you won't have the cost of the envelopes.

26. Do direct mail. In addition to mailing postcards here, there, and everywhere, obtain a targeted mailing list of people who would be interested in buying your cookbook, such as the subscribers to a food magazine, and send them a flyer. Contact the magazine to inquire about renting their subscriber list.

Three out of ten women collect cookbooks. Gear your flyer toward them, telling them why your cookbook will be a valuable addition to their kitchen. Make your flyer look like a book by folding the paper in half. Put your cookbook cover on the front, a recipe or two on the next page, a description of your cookbook and a list of the benefits and/or reasons why they will want to buy your cookbook on the third page—maybe use your back cover blurb for this—and ordering information on the back. You can also use this for prepub sales.

27. While you're doing the direct mail thing, rent targeted mailing lists and send your flyers to groups, organizations, and businesses who will be interested in purchasing your cookbook to either give or sell to their members, clients, and/or employees, or to use as a fundraiser. Design your flyer to appeal to them. Make sure your terms are on your flyer; also include a recipe card or two that shows a good sampling of all the great recipes in your cookbook.

28. Do a direct mailing to independent bookstores, retail stores, kitchen boutiques, and gift shops. Send a sell sheet with your terms and an overrun book cover. This mailing will let lots of bookstore owners know about your cookbook and will alert retailers who might be interested in offering it for sale in their stores. (See Appendix C for targeted mailing lists.)

The best time to do this kind of mailing is in March or August. In March, stores have big budgets and are looking for new books. In August, they're buying books for Christmas. Sending an overrun book cover with your sell sheet will increase your sales. They get hundreds of sell sheets every month but few include covers. Make yours stand out and be noticed. Tape or glue your sell sheet inside your overrun book cover and fold it in half to make it look like a book. You might also want to include a recipe card and a refrigerator magnet.

29. Give recipe cards to all the stores in your area, especially the bookstores and grocery stores. Ask them to put one in every customer's bag. Also give recipe cards to all your advertisers to give to their customers.

30. Leave a large stack of recipe cards and/or flyers in daycare centers, beauty shops, health clubs, and any other places you can think of where women will see your cookbook blurbs. Request permission from the manager before you do this. Eight-six percent of cookbook buyers are women.

31. Ask businesses to enclose your flyer in mailings they send to their clients. This is called piggy-backing and is also referred to as a co-op mailing. Offer to share the cost of postage.

32. Ask these same businesses to write an article, or to print one you've written, about your cookbook in their company newsletter. Make sure your ordering information is included.

33. Contact a local TV station or your PBS (Public Broadcasting Station) to interest them in doing an interview with you. Give a talk about creating your cookbook and/or do a cooking demonstration. Be sure to take a copy of your cookbook to show on the air. Give ordering instructions or say it's available in bookstores. Take a few extra copies to give to the host and the producer. When viewers call in requesting more information about your cookbook, they will enthusiastically promote it.

On channel 11 in Chicago, there is a show called Chicago Tonight which features people, places, and things in and around Chicago. Your area probably has a show like this, too. In San Antonio, there is a morning show called Great Day, SA which features local people and what they're doing.

34. Do radio interviews. Give cooking tips and short, easy recipes on the air. Tell funny stories about things that happened during the process of writing and publishing your cookbook. No one can see your cookbook on the radio but you can talk it up. Mention the title as often as you can without being obnoxious; every third or fourth sentence is good. Give information on how to order it. If you have a toll-free number, share it with the listeners or say the cookbook is available in bookstores. If it's a call-in show, offer a free cookbook as a prize to the tenth caller.

You can do radio shows from the convenience of your home, using your telephone. In addition to contacting local radio stations, get yourself and your cookbook listed in Bradley Communications' *Radio-TV Interview Report*, 800/553-8002, to show over 4,000 radio and television producers what you have to offer.

35. Do the deli. Team up with the owner to give a cooking demonstration on sandwiches and salads, using your recipes and their food. They'll advertise your appearance in advance, increasing customers for their store and their food, and for your cookbook.

36. Along those lines, do the bakery and make cookies. There are plenty of specialty food stores everywhere. Visit the ones in your area to set up demo's. Some grocery stores have a built-in kitchen on one of the aisles. You might even want to do a cooking demo at a restaurant.

37. Don't forget the coffee shop on crowded Saturday mornings. Talk to the manager and ask if you can demonstrate some recipes for muffins. (They have convection ovens for baking.) Give all the people there a bite of breakfast, along with a recipe card. They'll probably bite at buying your cookbook. Starbucks won't let you cook there but they are okay with you offering small samples that you've prepared ahead of time.

38. Microwave some cookbook magic by making your recipes in a microwave at a specialty store or a kitchen boutique that sells microwaves. Show their clientele how easy it is to adapt your recipes to microwave cooking.

39. Many stores which sell specific appliances have cooking classes that are well attended. You could be guest chef for the day. Bring lots of cookbooks to sell.

What small kitchen appliances work with your cookbook? How well does your cookbook incorporate cooking with them? Do you have recipes that require a food processor, bread machine, or ones that work well in a toaster oven? Do a cooking demo at a department store. They'll sell lots of appliances and you'll sell lots of cookbooks.

40. Partner with the Girl Scouts for their cookie sales. Set up a small table next to theirs to sell your cookbook. Offer them a generous portion of your proceeds. This works especially well if your cookbook is all about cookies. Be sure your cookbook is opened to the section on cookies for cookie buyers to look through. Ditto for the Boy Scouts and their candy sales.

41. Team up with Tupperware. Contact a local representative for Tupperware and offer to let them sell your cookbook in conjunction with their products at home parties. Give them the standard bookstore discount. Some Tupperware representatives also exhibit at arts and crafts shows.

Carry this a bit further. There are plenty of home parties where your cookbook will fit in nicely, such as cutlery and cookware parties. Go for home parties that women attend, like Avon, jewelry, and candle parties.

42. Many schools offer bake sales in connection with their fun fairs which are held once or twice a year. Bake a cake from a recipe in your cookbook to contribute to their cake walk. Offer your cookbook for sale on the side. Give the school a percentage of the profits.

43. Send a copy of your cookbook, with a cover letter, to Book Span, The Good Cook Book Club, 15 East 26th Street, 4th Floor, New York, NY 10010. Phone: 212/651-7400. Websites: www.bookspan.com and www.thegoodcook.com. If your cookbook is selected, you could sell thousands of copies.

44. Offer your cookbook as a premium to local banks, insurance agencies, and other companies and corporations in your area for

them to give as a gift to entice new clients. They will buy your cookbook in quantity. Give them a nice discount, 50% off the cover price.

45. Along those same lines, offer quantities of your cookbook to local Realtors and apartment complexes for them to give as a gift to new home buyers and renters. Give them the same discount, 50% off the cover price.

46. Offer your cookbook to all the extended stay hotels across the country for sale to their temporary residents. Thousands upon thousands of people stay for several weeks or months and they may have forgotten to pack a cookbook. They'll be so pleased that you were considerate enough to place your cookbook there for sale.

Call the hotels in your area to get the phone number and address for their corporate office. Call the headquarters to briefly pitch your project and to inquire about the procedure for sending your cookbook for consideration. Be sure to get a contact name. Give them the standard bookstore discount.

47. Offer your cookbook to a school, church, or charitable organization in your community for them to use as a fundraiser. Give them a great discount or offer to let them share the cost of your print run. This is beneficial for both of you. Here's how it works: You print more copies at a lower unit price. You split the cost and copies with them. You have your cookbooks to sell at a lower cost to you and they have cookbooks for their fundraiser.

48. Get a good buzz going about your cookbook. Buzz is a term used in the publishing industry to create interest in a book. It's simply word of mouth and it is extraordinarily powerful. Ask your friends, family, co-workers, neighbors, and everyone else you know, to talk about your cookbook to everyone they know.

This soon creates a ripple effect and people everywhere will want to buy your cookbook. They'll walk into bookstores in different states and ask for your cookbook. If it's not on the shelf, they'll order it from the bookstore. Soon the bookstores will start ordering multiple copies from you or your distributor.

49. Put up a full-color poster of your cookbook cover and ordering information in the break room at work. Place a plate of goodies with a stack of recipe cards next to it. Keep lots of cookbooks in your

desk drawer for all your co-workers who will come running to your desk wanting two or three copies each. Have all your friends or the people in your organization do the same.

50. Showcase your cookbook on your website and on many other websites. Create cooperative links with other websites. If you don't have a website, create one. Make it colorful and informative. Post some of your recipes that can be downloaded. Change them every week or so to keep visitors coming back to your website. People who surf the web will visit your site, decide they want your cookbook, and buy it.

If you're not set up to collect money with credit cards, link your cookbook to www.amazon.com, www.bn.com, www.borders.com, and/or www.booksamillion.com. Make sure these cyber shops are showcasing your cookbook. In addition to having your cookbook on these sites, you'll also earn a referral fee if you've joined the affiliate program.

51. Get your cookbook featured in cookbook catalogs and other related catalogs. Many catalog companies also do book reviews and offer distribution. (See Appendix B.)

52. Attend all the community festivals, street fairs, the Memorial Day, 4th of July, and Labor Day festivals in your area. Rent booth space from the sponsor. Set up a table and sell your cookbook. Give recipe cards to everyone who comes by. These festivals and fairs abound in every community.

53. In almost every town, all across America, there is a chili cook-off. It's usually held in conjunction with the 4th of July festivities. Of course you'll want to enter, using a recipe for chili from your cookbook. When you win the contest, you can share your secret recipe. Even if you don't win, you can still share it. Walk around and give a recipe card, with your prize-winning chili recipe, to everyone there. Invite them over to your booth to buy your cookbook.

54. Rent booth space at arts and crafts fairs to sell your cookbook. Display your poster prominently. Glue it to cardboard backing and place it on an easel or tape it on the wall behind you. Set your table decoratively with a lacy tablecloth to look like a dining table.

Do a nice arrangement with candles, fresh flowers, and copies of your cookbook.

Serve your cookbook for sale. Open one of your cookbooks to show the recipes. Due to fire regulations, you probably won't be able to light the candles but they'll still set a festive mood and add to the perceived value of your cookbook. Give everyone who stops at your booth a refrigerator magnet.

Most sponsors of arts and crafts fairs request an item for their raffle. Donate one of your cookbooks. Place lots of flyers and/or recipe cards on the raffle table where tickets are sold for attendees to pick up. This will help draw them to your booth.

Some arts and crafts fairs will let you sample food if you have insurance. Sampling ready-made recipes will increase the volume of traffic to your booth and dramatically increase cookbook sales.

55. Offer a gift with your cookbook. Tie a set of measuring spoons with a decorative ribbon to the plastic comb binding. If your cookbook is perfect bound or a 3-ring binder, offer something special related to cooking and your cookbook. People respond well to buying something when there's a free gift involved.

Instead of selling your cookbook by itself, create a gift basket which includes your cookbook, kitchen items, and a few food treats, such as fresh fruit, candy, or cookies.

56. Do a lemonade stand like you did when you were a child. Get your kids, and some of the neighborhood kids, involved. Along with homemade lemonade and lemon cookies you've made from your recipes, sell your cookbook to all the adults who wander by with their children.

57. If a lemonade stand isn't your style, have a tea party. Rent the community center. Be very British about it. Serve high tea and scones, along with your cookbook, in the middle of the afternoon. Charge a small admittance fee to cover the cost of your food and the community center rental. Schedule it well in advance so that it will be listed on the community calendar of events and in the community newsletter, which is sent to every resident. This also gives you free advertising all over town for your cookbook. The people who aren't able to attend may go to a bookstore and buy your cookbook.

58. Go to a sidewalk cafe where there are lots of people. Order lunch or coffee and sell your cookbook there. You may or may not be able to do this. Talk to the proprietor first to get permission. Convince him or her by saying that selling your cookbook there will create quite a commotion, drawing people to see what you're doing. When they see a cookbook, they'll decide they're hungry, go inside and buy lunch, then come back out and buy your cookbook.

59. Go for sidewalk sales. These are week-long events held during the summer. Choose a store that will be conducive to cookbook sales. Ask the owner if you can set up a table to sell your cookbook. Mention that your cookbook will draw additional customers to his/her storefront. Offer to pay a table fee or a percentage of sales.

60. Send out a press release every time you want coverage for an upcoming event, to announce something special about your cookbook, or something you're involved in relating to your cookbook. Don't overdo it, though; if you blitz the media, they won't blitz you.

61. Host a buffet luncheon or a dinner party with food made from some of your recipes. Rent a hall with kitchen facilities and make a fabulous meal. Charge admission to cover the cost of your food; $5.00 for lunch, $8.00 for dinner. Have your cookbook there for sale. After everyone eats your delicious food, they'll want to buy your cookbook. Another way to do this is to charge a higher admission that includes your cookbook.

62. Let's not forget breakfast. Everyone should start their day with a good breakfast. Contact your local school or Kiwanis Club to find out when they are having a pancake breakfast. Ask the sponsor if you can sell your cookbook there, giving the organization a percentage of your profits. (Here in San Antonio, we have a taco breakfast.) Sell your cookbook at breakfast to start everyone's day off right.

63. Instead of having a garage sale, have a cookbook yard sale. Set up tables on your front lawn for food samples and your cookbooks. Place posters, balloons, and ribbons to direct traffic to your house. You may have to get a garage sale permit for this.

64. If you live in an apartment, rent the clubhouse. Have a cookbook sale, along with free samples of food—appetizers or small tid-

bits—for all your neighbors. Post colorful invitations around the apartment complex. Most clubhouses have lots of tables and chairs you can set up. The complex will either let the resident use the clubhouse for free or charge a modest fee.

65. Get a permit for a picnic in the park and pray it doesn't rain. Invite the entire community. Get all your friends, or the people in your group or organization, to help you. Either do a barbecue or set up several tables with fried chicken, potato salad, corn on the cob, cookies, and other food you've made from your recipes to sell to all the people who attend. Set up one table in the center of it all to sell your cookbook. Go all out. Make it a day. Have games and do all the things that make picnics fun.

66. Do food festivals. They are held just about everywhere in your neighborhood and the metropolitan area around you. Set up a table and sell your cookbook, along with food you've made from your recipes. Get into the spirit of things. If it's a Greek festival, make gyros. If it's a German fest, make German potato salad or serve bratwurst and sauerkraut. If it's Chinese, make egg rolls or dim sum. If it's an apple fest, make apple pie. If it's a strawberry festival, make strawberry shortcake.

67. Post colorful notices about your cookbook, with information on how to buy it, on all the bulletin boards around town in grocery stores, libraries, arts and crafts stores, and many other places. If you can, also leave a large stack of recipe cards.

68. Carry a couple of cookbooks with you at all times. You never know who you'll run into. When you start talking about your cookbook, the person will probably want to buy one. This works equally well with acquaintances and strangers. This is referred to as trunk sales because you're selling your cookbook from the trunk of your car.

69. Enclose a flyer or a recipe card in every bill you pay and in every letter you write. Don't be shy.

70. Ask your local cable company, water company, gas company, telephone company, and electric company to enclose a cookbook coupon or flyer with the monthly bill sent to their customers.

71. Get in on a co-op coupon mailing which is sent to thousands of local households. Contact Valpak at 800/660-5025 or visit their website at www.valpak.com. In lieu of a coupon mailing, get in on the grocery store flyer mailing.

72. Enclose recipe cards with all the greeting cards you send, especially Christmas cards. Hit on all the holidays and days that aren't holidays, like St. Patrick's Day. Send Christmas cards early so people will have time to order your cookbook to give as gifts. Mention that cookbooks, especially yours, make a wonderful present. Thanksgiving and Mother's Day are also great for cookbook sales.

73. Have a holiday all your own for your cookbook. Pick a date and name it after your cookbook. Of course you'll want to get the local media involved. You are creating a holiday, even if it is only in your community. That's certainly major news. You might want to do this when sales begin to dwindle. It will spark new interest in your cookbook.

74. Who says you can't invent two holidays? Space the second one about six months after your first one. People might still remember the first one, so don't call the second one a holiday. Call it a day. Tie it into a theme with a recipe from your cookbook. Have a Meatloaf Monday, Taco Tuesday, Wellington Wednesday, Teriyaki Thursday, Fishy Friday, Spaghetti Saturday, or Stir-Fry Sunday. Send out a press release with your recipe-of-the-day and the day and date this event falls on.

75. Many community colleges and universities sponsor book fairs. Rent a table and sell your cookbook. San Antonio College has their annual book fair outdoors the first Saturday in April and they love authors. They will give you a free table under a tent. Plenty of other organizations hold book fairs throughout the year. Contact your local chamber of commerce to find out who sponsors them, and where and when they will be held.

If your cookbook is health related, find out where and when the health and wellness fairs are in your area. Rent a table and sell your cookbook, touting its health benefits to everyone who stops by. Check with community colleges and health organizations to find the sponsors for these events.

76. If you like to travel, or are going on vacation, and want to promote your cookbook on tour, contact the colleges and universities where you will be visiting to find out when their book fairs are scheduled.

77. Before you get there or while you're there, contact out-of-town bookstores, gift shops, and other retail locations where your cookbook will fit in nicely. Give the manager a sell sheet, show him or her your cookbook, and talk to him/her about carrying it. If you contact them beforehand, arrange personal appearances—book signings and cooking demonstrations.

For a directory of bookstores, go to www.bookweb.org. This website includes addresses and web sites for bookstores. Also visit www.bn.com, www.booksamillion.com, and www.borders.com. to locate their bookstores where you will be traveling. Another helpful website to locate out-of-town bookstores is www.booksense.com.

78. In addition to school and community sponsored book fairs, there are numerous other book fairs you can attend. The St. Petersburg Times in Tampa, Florida has a huge book fair in November at Polk County College. Several weeks after that, Miami hosts the Miami International Book Fair. Chicago has its three-day outdoor Printer's Row in June, to name a few.

You can find a list of book fairs by going to the library and looking in *Literary Market Place*. LMP, as it's called for short, is a huge reference volume which contains information about all aspects of the publishing industry. The list of book fairs is not an all-inclusive, comprehensive list; it shows the major ones. (See Appendix C for more information on book fairs.)

Contact the chamber of commerce and the visitor's and convention bureau where you will be traveling six months in advance to find out what's coming up in their area. Get contact information for the sponsor. Call and request a registration form or ask to be put on their mailing list.

79. If you're of a mind to, and your budget is big enough, exhibit at book trade shows. These are non-selling events but the exposure you get for your cookbook is very valuable. The biggest and best is Book Expo, held annually the first weekend in June. It moves from

New York to Los Angeles in alternate years. The price for a booth in the writer's row section is $1,600.00.

Call Reed Exhibitions at 800/840-5614 and ask for an exhibitor packet. Website: www.bookexpoamerica.com. You can show off your cookbook to the 30,000+ booksellers and other industry professionals that attend. Be prepared to hand out lots of flyers and to give away autographed copies of your cookbook. Booksellers will write orders for your cookbook and many other wonderful things can happen.

Several years ago, a self-published cookbook author exhibited in the small press section. Crate & Barrel ordered 50,000 copies. This is one of the success stories. It doesn't happen often but happens often enough to give one hope.

Another good reason to exhibit is that large publishing houses occasionally pick up self-published books, offering a nice advance and a large print run for books that have a proven market and documented sales of 10,000 or more. Sometimes they offer to publish just because they like the book. While you're at Book Expo, be sure to attend the Cookbook Expo.

80. If your budget isn't big enough, you can still exhibit at trade shows. Several organizations geared for small press publishers provide a group book exhibit. They'll showcase your cookbook for a fee, usually around $125.00, and list it in their catalog which is given to show attendees. (See Appendix C for a list of book exhibitors.)

81. If your cookbook is suitable for library sales, exhibit at the American Library Association conferences held throughout the year in various locations. Contact them at 50 East Huron Street, Chicago, IL 60611. Phone: 312/944-6780 or 800/545-2433. Website: www.ala.org.

82. While we're on the subject of shows, there are numerous gift shows held throughout the country where you can show and sell mega copies of your cookbook. The Orlando International Gift Show is held in January. The Las Vegas Gourmet Housewares Show is held in May. The Atlanta International Gift & Home Furnishings Market is held in January and July. (See Appendix C for a list of trade and gift shows.)

83. A slight twist on this is to exhibit at conferences, conventions, and trade shows that are conducive to cookbook sales. The American Culinary Federation National Convention is held in Washington, D.C. in July. The International Association of Culinary Professionals holds its convention in April in Dallas. There are many other regional and national shows where your cookbook will fit in nicely.

To find out what's coming up in your area, contact your local chamber of commerce or the visitor's and convention bureau. Also look in the yellow pages under associations, convention information, and convention services and facilities. Call the appropriate ones to find out where and when their next trade show is. (To locate out-of-town conventions, see Appendix C.)

84. If there aren't any regional shows, conferences, or conventions in your area, start one. Team up with individuals, organizations, and businesses in your community to create your own one-of-a-kind Cooking Convention. Talk with businesses who have products that will complement cookbooks, such as kitchenware boutiques, grocery stores, restaurants, delicatessens, bakeries, and sandwich shops.

Stretch a little. Think of everything that is in some way connected with food and cooking. The local flower shop may wish to participate, showcasing their floral arrangements on a dining table setting, along with their business cards and brochures. Stretch a little more. Realtors and banks may want to exhibit there. Kitchen remodeling businesses may also be interested. Situate yourself in the center of activities to get lots of attention and to sell lots of cookbooks.

85. Have your cookbook cover printed on T-shirts. If you belong to a group or organization, have all the members wear them whenever they go out (between launderings, of course). Give some T-shirts to your family and friends. Whenever you, and everyone else, wears the T-shirts, be sure to carry copies of your cookbook to sell.

Having your book cover on T-shirts is much more common than you may think. Many authors do it, mostly from pride and partly for advertising. Look under screen printing in the yellow pages to find local places that print T-shirts or see the listings in Appendix C for promotional products.

86. Wear your T-shirt at all the book shows and everywhere else you go to promote and sell your cookbook. Offer a free T-shirt to anyone who buys 3 copies of your cookbook. This incentive will help you sell multiple copies. If you run out of T-shirts, or even if you don't, offer a buy three cookbooks, get one free sale.

87. Do a cookbook kiosk. Many shopping malls have kiosk stands you can rent in the middle of the mall. The traffic is already there. Approach all the people walking through the mall, give them a recipe card and invite them to your kiosk to look at your cookbook. Once they see it, they'll want to buy it. Increase your sales by offering kitchen and cooking-related items.

88. Add merchandising to the mix. Refrigerator magnets, jar openers, pot holders, coffee cups, kitchen towels, and tote bags can be printed with your cookbook cover and contact information, such as your toll-free number or website. All these items help promote your cookbook. The less expensive ones are great as giveaways to every person who buys your cookbook.

You can sell your coordinated merchandise in addition to your cookbook at farmer's and flea markets, arts and crafts shows, book fairs, food festivals, gift shows, and practically everywhere else you go to promote and sell your cookbook. (See Appendix C for places where you can order these items.)

If your budget allows for only one item, make that one item a refrigerator magnet. It's the best way to keep your product in front of all your potential buyers. Give it to everyone you meet. They'll put it on their fridge and see it several times a day.

89. Many shopping malls have special weekend events where you can rent a table or booth and sell your cookbook. Crossroads Mall in San Antonio has a Sample the Southwest weekend in November. For events that are centered around food, decorate your booth to fit the theme. Contact the malls in your area to see what events they have planned.

If you'd rather not rent a booth, partner with one of the exhibitors who are offering food. Ask them to place your cookbook in their booth; give them the standard bookstore discount or offer to share the space and cost of the booth.

90. Approach furniture stores. Suggest that they place copies of your cookbook on some, or all, of the dining room tables, or on a shelf in the hutches. Ask them to also place copies next to the cashier's office. Make it easy for them. Provide a dump for your cookbooks. A dump is a cardboard display stand that holds multiple copies of your cookbook.

91. Go a bit further with this. Contact department stores, such as Sears and J. C. Penney, that carry dining room furniture and kitchen items. Have them place your cookbook in both areas and at the cash register in each department.

92. Don't stop there. Contact warehouse home improvement centers, such as Home Depot and Lowe's. Have them place your cookbook on the kitchen counter displays and next to the cash register.

93. Along those same lines, look in your local phone book under kitchen remodeling. Contact the owners and suggest a premium—a free cookbook to their clients when they remodel their kitchen. Offer them a 50% discount. If they're not into buying in bulk from you, ask the owners to give your flyer to customers, or ask to rent their customer list and do a mailing yourself.

If they have a brochure which features their cabinetry and counters, suggest that they use your cookbook as a prop when they design their next brochure. This is great advertising for your cookbook, nestled comfortably and naturally in a kitchen setting.

94. Send a cookbook to school with your kid during Teacher Appreciation Week to give to the teacher, along with flyers for the teacher to give to other teachers. Keep on going. Contact the principal to see if the school will send your cookbook flyers home with all the kids to give to their parents. Offer the school $2.00 or $3.00 for every cookbook sold. Have the school be the pick-up place or send the cookbooks home with the kids.

95. In lieu of that, or in addition to it, show up at the PTA meeting with lots of cookbooks and flyers. At the very least, you'll sell a large number of cookbooks to the parents. The best time to do this is in October or early November; suggest that cookbooks make wonderful Christmas presents.

96. Have a calendar printed up featuring a special recipe for each month. This will keep your cookbook in front of all the people and businesses you give it to, and it can be a profitable sideline. It's also a nice thank you gift to give to everyone who helped with your cookbook.

97. Your local library is a great resource for information about publishing and marketing your cookbook, and is also a great avenue to showcase your cookbook. Contact the librarians who were so helpful during the creation of your cookbook and schedule a lecture there. They'll love to see the finished product; some libraries will let you sell your cookbook after your talk.

98. Most community colleges and universities have a culinary arts program. Some of the students enrolled in these courses belong to a culinary arts club. They do fundraisers several times a year at various school functions, selling food they've prepared. Offer your cookbook as a fundraiser item for them; give them $3.00 for every cookbook sold.

99. Enter your cookbook in contests for awards and prizes. When your cookbook wins, have gold stickers printed with the name of the award; put them on the front cover of your cookbook. Award-winning cookbooks will get more attention from the media, book-store owners, libraries, and distributors. (See Appendix B for cook-book contests.)

100. Advertise your cookbook in the food section in newspapers and in magazines like *Bon Appetit, Fine Cooking*, and *Gourmet*, as well as in *Good Housekeeping, Redbook, Better Homes and Gardens*, and *Ladies' Home Journal*. This can be a bit pricey, but if your budget allows it, showcase your cookbook where thousands of people will see it.

In lieu of advertising, which may or may not give you a good return, many of the above-mentioned magazines might do a free blurb on your cookbook if you send it in for review. They also have columns and departments that are looking for filler material. You can always send in a recipe and provide information about your cook-book. You might want to pick up a copy of these magazines to see where your cookbook will fit in. (See Appendix D and Appendix F for a list of magazines.)

101. Show and sell mega copies of your cookbook on TV. Get on QVC and the Home Shopping Network. Visit their websites at www.qvc.com and www.hsn.com.

There are many more than 101 ways to sell your cookbook. Here's another one: Do a second cookbook. Place an ad in the local newspaper calling for recipes or send a press release announcing the creation of your new cookbook. Maybe the paper will interview you again.

Be sure to mention your first cookbook and say that copies are still available. Since it was such a huge success in your community—it's probably a household name by now—you'll get lots of contributors for your second cookbook. And if, by some remote chance, someone has not yet heard of your cookbook, they'll certainly want to buy a copy and get in on the action the next time around.

This list only scratches the surface to help you get started selling your cookbook. Use your creativity and your imagination. The possibilities are endless. Get together with your friends and family, or with the people in your group or organization, who are going to help you sell your cookbook and have a brainstorming session or two. You can cook up at least 101 more ways to sell your cookbook.

Best wishes and congratulations on being a cookbook author!

Appendix A

Cookbook Printers

A list of cookbook printers, how to contact them, and the base price for their minimum print run, follows. Most will typeset your recipes or you can submit them camera-ready, press-ready, or online. Four-color covers, full color dividers, and binding are included in their base price. They offer various items and upgrades for additional charges. Visit their websites for more information or call to request an information packet.

The Cookbook Company, www.cookbookco.com

    50 cookbooks with up to 150 recipes is $5.45
    100 cookbooks with up to 150 recipes is $3.35
    200 cookbooks with up to 150 recipes is $2.45

Cookbook Publishers, www.cookbookpublishers.com

    100 cookbooks with up to 150 recipes is $4.40
    200 cookbooks with up to 150 recipes is $2.85

Favorite Recipes Press, www.frpbooks.com

    Favorite Recipes Press has a minimum print run of 2,500 cookbooks; they quote prices based on number of pages and design options. They also offer distribution, marketing, and promotional services.

Fundcraft Publishing, www.fundcraft.com

Fundcraft offers Internet advertising and a community cookbook awards program. They also offer on-demand printing with a 25-book minimum at their affiliated website, www.instantpublisher.com.

200 cookbooks with up to 150 recipes is $2.65

G & R Publishing Company, www.cookbookprinting.com

100 cookbooks with up to 150 recipes is $4.30
200 cookbooks with up to 150 recipes is $3.05

Gateway Publishing, www.gatebook.com

50 cookbooks with up to 100 recipes is $6.93
150 cookbooks with up to 100 recipes is $3.77

Jumbo Jack's Cookbooks, www.jumbojacks.com

Visit their website to request an information packet and price chart.

Morris Press Cookbooks, www.morriscookbooks.com

Morris Press Cookbooks has printed several of my cookbooks. They offer Internet advertising and a community cookbook awards program.

200 cookbooks with up to 150 recipes is $2.60

Rasmussen Company, www.cookbookprinter.com

Prices are given upon request.

~~~~~~~~~~~~~~~~~~~~~~~~~

Wimmer Cookbooks, 4650 Shelby Air Drive, Memphis, TN 38118. Phone: 800/548-2537. Website: www.wimmerco.com

Wimmer Cookbooks has two printing packages. The designer series is a minimum print run of 1,000 cookbooks with comb binding; the custom series is a minimum print run of 3,000 cookbooks with concealed wire binding; they quote prices based on number of pages and design options. Some of their services include Internet and catalog advertising, storage and fulfillment services, and cookbook exhibits at trade conventions and gift shows.

Appendix B

Cookbook Contests /
Catalogs / Conferences

There are many contests, both regional and national, that you can enter your cookbook in. The following is a list of major cookbook awards. To find more cookbook contests, look in LMP in the Awards and Prizes section. To find regional awards in your area, check with your librarian or do a Google search.

Cookbook Contests

Given by the Publishers Marketing Association, the *Benjamin Franklin Award* recognizes excellence in independent publishing. Publications, grouped by genre, are judged on editorial and design merit by top practitioners in each field. Trophies are awarded to the best books in several categories. Website: www.pma-online.org.

ForeWord Magazine's *Book of the Year Award* was established to bring increased attention from librarians and booksellers to the achievements of independent publishers and their authors. A jury of librarians, booksellers, and reviewers are selected to judge the fifty categories for entry; they select winners and finalists based on editorial excellence and professional production as well as originality of the narrative and the value the book adds to its genre. Website: www.forewordmagazine.com.

Given by the International Association of Culinary Professionals, the *IACP Cookbook Award* (formerly the Julia Child Cookbook Award) honors the first cookbook by a writer who has not previously authored or co-authored a cookbook. Website: www.iacp.com.

The *Independent Book Publisher Awards* are designed to bring increased recognition to the deserving, but often unsung, titles published by independent authors and publishers in fifty different categories. Website: www.independentpublisher.com.

The James Beard Foundation presents the *James Beard Award* each year in fifteen categories for food and beverage books published in the U.S and Canada. The award recipients are selected by more than 600 food and beverage industry professionals. Winners receive a bronze medallion engraved with the image of James Beard, the late cookbook author, chef, and cooking teacher. Website: www.jamesbeard.org.

Nonprofit cookbooks that have sold over 100,000 copies, regardless of when they were published, are eligible for the *Walter S. McIlhenny Hall of Fame*, honoring books considered classics in the field.

The *Tabasco Community Cookbook Awards* (for nonprofits) were established on behalf of the McIlhenny Company as a way to recognize achievements in the area of community cookbooks and to encourage the preservation of regional food traditions. It recognizes the best of the thousands of cookbooks issued annually to generate money for charitable causes. Cash donations are made to the charities specified by three national and six regional award winners. Website: www.tabasco.com.

Writer's Digest magazine offers *Writer's Digest National Self-Published Book Awards* for the best self-published book in nine categories. Website: www.writersdigest.com.

There are numerous other cookbook awards, including the Gourmand World Cookbook Fair Awards, Small Press Award, Mid-America Publishing Association Cookbook Awards, AJLI Best Fundraiser, Best Community Service Project in US, Southern Books Competition, and Best New BBQ Book, to name a few.

Catalogs and Newsletters

There are plenty of catalogs to get your cookbook listed in. Your distributor will include your cookbook in their catalog which is mailed to bookstores, given to booksellers at trade shows, and taken by sales reps into the stores. Your cookbook will also be featured in catalogs prepared by book exhibitors for trade shows.

To place your cookbook in a multitude of catalogs, look through *The Catalog of Catalogs* to find ones suitable for your cookbook. You can order a copy by calling 800/331-8355. Also look through the *Shop at Home Catalog Directory*, which showcases over 600 mail-order catalogs. 7100 E. Bellview Avenue, Suite 305, Greenwood Village, CO 80311. Phone: 303/843-0302.

The Directory of Mail Order Catalogs, *Directory of Business to Business Catalogs*, and *Mail Order Business Directory*, available at your public library, will give you plenty of food for thought about the catalogs that would be receptive to your cookbook. Don't overlook the obvious. Look through catalogs you receive at home and at work to determine if they would be appropriate for your cookbook.

The Cookbook Collectors' Exchange is a bimonthly newsletter sent to 7,500 cookbook collectors. You can buy advertising space and have your cookbook reviewed. Contact Sue Erwin, The Cookbook Collectors' Exchange, P.O Box 89, Magalia, CA 95954. Phone: 530/873-4311.

Cookbooks Unlimited is the monthly newsletter of the Cookbook Collector's Club. Contact Barbara Gelink, Cookbooks Unlimited, dba Otento Books, 4756 Terrace Drive, San Diego, CA 92116-2514. Phone: 619/281-8962.

Conferences

There are a variety of culinary conferences you can attend to learn more about food and cooking, to see what's hot, and to discover what's new. There are also two cookbook conferences, offered by cookbook-specific printers, designed especially for cookbook authors.

FRP Cookbook University is held annually in Nashville, TN. This 2-day school offers a variety of courses designed for cookbook authors. Contact Julee Clark at 800/358-0560. www.frpbooks.com.

IACP, The International Association of Culinary Professionals holds several conferences and conventions every year, as well as offering a newsletter for members which includes cookbook reviews. Website: www.iacp.com.

Wimmer Cookbook Publishing Seminar is held annually in Memphis, TN. This 2-1/2 day workshop offers cookbook authors an array of information about publishing and promoting a cookbook. Website: www.wimmerco.com.

Writer's Colony. While this isn't a conference, they offer a number of residencies for writers, including several for food writers. Website: www.writerscolony.org.

Appendix C

Websites for Recipes / Promotions / Book Fairs / Trade and Gift Shows

Here are websites where you can obtain recipes and cooking information, cyber shops to showcase your cookbook, sites for marketing information, places for promotional materials and related culinary items, as well as information for exhibiting your cookbook at various trade and gift shows.

Recipes / Cooking Information

Look through the following websites for more than recipes. Many of them offer cooking hints and tips, guides to nutrition, substitutions, and much more. Some offer a place to show and sell your cookbook.

www.allrecipes.com
www.americastestkitchen.com
Better Homes & Gardens: www.bhg.com
www.ciaoitalia.com
www.cooks.com
www.cooking.com
The Cook's Thesaurus: www.switcheroo.com
www.culinary.net
www.eatingwell.com
www.epicurious.com
www.foodfit.com
The Food Network: www.foodtv.com
www.globalgourmet.com
www.kitchenlink.com
Kraft Interactive Kitchen: www.kraftfoods.com

www.mealtime.org
www.myrecipes.com
www.pbs.org/everydayfood
www.recipe.com
www.reciperewards.com
www.recipezaar.com
www.sallys-place.com
Veggies Unite: www.vegweb.com

Internet Promotions

To help promote and sell your cookbook, get it seen everywhere you can on the Internet. Many sites offer a free listing and are a good place to start. Visit www.authorsden.com, www.redroom.com, and www.authortree.com for free author pages where you can showcase your cookbook and promote it online. Most states have at least one privately owned website dedicated to the sale of locally made products and services, including cookbooks. Go to www.shopbystate.com to search for online stores in your state.

Showcase your cookbook on the online bookstores listed in Chapter Seven. Surf the web to find more. They are popping up practically overnight. The best place to show and sell your cookbook is your own website. You can create a website for free or next to nothing. The best ones I've found are: www.tripod.lycos.com and www.freewebs.com.

Marketing Information

To help market and promote your cookbook, check out these two websites: www.bookmarket.com offers helpful tips for marketing books and useful links to publishing websites. www.gmarketing.com provides helpful resources to help you successfully market your book.

Direct Mail

In addition to promoting your cookbook on the Internet, direct mail is a way to reach thousands of people who will be interested in buying your cookbook. To find targeted mailing lists, look through

LMP, which has a list of mailing list brokers and services. Research the following websites and catalogs which provide detailed information. Your local librarian can help you find targeted mailing lists for your area.

Direct Marketing Market Place is updated annually and available in your local library. It lists leading direct-marketing companies, major service firms, suppliers, and organizations.

Reed Business Information has a database of 250,000 names and addresses which is updated monthly. Phone: 800/537-7930. Website: www.dm2lists.com.

The American Booksellers Association (ABA), 200 White Plains Road, Tarrytown, NY 10591, is a gold mine for targeted mailing lists to bookstores. Visit www.bookweb.org or call them at 800/637-0037 to inquire about renting one of their specific mailing lists. You'll probably be interested in the one that targets bookstores that carry cookbooks.

American Business Information, 5711 South 86th Circle, P.O. Box 27347, Omaha, NE 68127, has a database of 11 million business addresses. Request a free catalog which will provide information on specific lists. Phone: 800/321-0869. Website: www.infoUSA.com.

Promotional Products

Promotional materials, such as kitchen towels, T-shirts, potholders, coffee cups, refrigerator magnets, and other culinary items to coordinate with your cookbook, will help your cookbook be noticed and stand out from the crowd.

Infinite Ideas offers promotional products including culinary items. Phone: 901/754-7799. Website: www.advertisingitems.com.

Quill has a promotional products catalog featuring T-shirts, coffee cups, refrigerator magnets, and more. Phone: 800/982-3400. Website: www.quill.com.

Twig One Stop prints flyers, address labels, and brochures. They also offer magnets, mugs, and other promotional items. Phone: 561/740-9901. Website: www.twigonestop.com.

4imprint offers thousands of promotional products. Phone: 888/234-5797. Website: www.4imprint.com.

Vista Print offers business cards, refrigerator magnets, T-shirts, mugs, and other promotional items. Website: www.vistaprint.com.

Cafe Press offers T-shirts, calendars, posters, mugs, and more. Plus you can set up shop here to sell your stuff. Website: www.cafepress.com.

Book Fairs

Book fairs are a great place to showcase and sell your cookbook. Several are particularly friendly to cookbook authors and feature cooking demonstrations: Baltimore Book Festival, Fall for the Book Literary Festival, Miami Book Fair International, and the Texas Book Festival. For a full list of book fairs, as well as other useful information about author venues, go to www.booktv.org and click on Book Fairs.

Arizona Book Festival celebrates the Southwest in Phoenix, AZ. Phone: 602/712-1256. Website: www.azbookfestival.org.

Baltimore Book Festival offers readings and talks by authors, and cooking demonstrations. Phone: 410/837-4636. www.bop.org.

Border Book Festival is a weeklong festival in Las Cruces, New Mexico which includes writers, artists and storytellers, vendors, panels and workshops, readings and performances. Phone: 505/523-3988. Website: www.borderbookfestival.org.

Fall for the Book Literary Festival in Fairfax, VA is a street festival which includes storytellers, author talks, and cooking demonstrations. Phone: 703/993-3986. Website: www.fallforthebook.org.

Miami Book Fair International is a week-long fair of author events, cooking demonstrations, and children's activities. Phone: 305/237-3258. Website: www.miamibookfair.com.

Printer's Row Book Fair in Chicago is a three-day outdoor event. I can vouch for this one; it's a great place to sell cookbooks. I attended for several years when I lived in Chicago. Phone: 312/987-9896. Website: www.printersrowbookfair.org.

San Francisco Bay Area Book Festival offers readings, lectures, and vendors. Phone: 415/487-4550.

St. Petersburg Times Festival of Reading offers author events. Phone: 727/893-8481. Website: www.festivalofreading.com.

Texas Book Festival in Austin features author lectures and readings, as well as cookbook author events. I can also vouch for this one. I've been attending ever since I moved to San Antonio. Phone: 512/477-4055. Website: www.texasbookfestival.org.

Trade and Gift Shows

In addition to Book Expo and the American Library Association Conferences, you might like to exhibit your cookbook at other regional trade and gift shows, culinary conferences, and related conventions to increase exposure and sales for your cookbook. The following are just a few of the major gift and trade shows where you can show and sell your cookbook.

ASD/AMD Trade Show, Las Vegas, NV; also held in New York. Phone: 800/421-4511. Website: www.merchandisegroup.com.

Atlanta Spring/Fall Immediate Delivery Show and The Spring/Fall Atlanta International Gift and Home Furnishings Market, Atlanta, GA. Phone: 800/285-6278. www.americasmart.com.

California Gift Show, Los Angeles, CA. Phone: 800/272-7469. Website: www.californiagiftshow.com.

Louisville Gift Show, Louisville, KY and St. Louis Gift Show in Collinsville, IL. 513/861-1139. www.louisvillegiftshow.com.

Mountains and Plains Booksellers Association Trade Show, Denver, CO. Phone: 800/752-0249. www.mountainsplains.org.

National Nutritional Foods Association, Las Vegas, NV. Phone: 800/966-6632. Website: www.nnfa.org.

New York International Gift Fair, New York, NY. Phone: 800/272-7469. Website: www.nyigf.com.

Orlando Gift Show, Orlando, FL. Phone: 800/318-2238. Website: www.orlandogiftshow.com.

Philadelphia Gift Show, Fort Washington, PA. Phone: 678/285-3976. Website: www.urban-expo.com.

Portland Gift and Accessories Show, Portland, OR. Phone: 800/346-1212. Website: www.portlandgift.com.

San Francisco International Gift Fair, San Francisco, CA. Phone: 800/346-1212. Website: www.sfigf.com.

Seattle Gift Show, Seattle, WA. Phone: 800/346-1212. Website: www.seattlegift.com.

Southern Independent Booksellers Alliance Trade Show, Orlando, FL. Phone: 803/779-0118. Website: www.sibaweb.com.

Summer Craftsmen's Fair, Gatlinburg, TN. Phone: 865/436-7479. Website: www.craftsmenfair.com.

Look through the *Encyclopedia of Associations*, available at your library, to find organizations which hold trade conferences and conventions that would be appropriate to showcase your cookbook. Contact the likely ones to find out where and when their conference is.

Combined Book Exhibits

If you don't want to rent space on your own, the following companies offer a combined book exhibit where your cookbook will be shown, along with many other books.

Association Book Exhibit, 9423 Old Mount Vernon Road, Alexandria, VA 22309. 703/619-5030. www.bookexhibit.com. They attend major book and library shows.

Combined Book Exhibits. They attend major book and library shows. Phone: 800/462-7687. Website: www.combinedbook.com.

Quality and Unique (library distributors) also offer book exhibits. Contact them to inquire about their services. (See Chapter Seven.) If you have a bookstore distributor, ask them to display your cookbook and include it in their conference catalog. There may be a fee for this service.

Scott Flora, The Small Publishers Association of North America (SPAN), 1618 West Colorado Avenue, Colorado Springs, CO 80904. Phone: 719/475-1726. Website: www.spannet.org. In addition to exhibiting at book and library trade shows, they offer co-op advertising, a monthly newsletter of marketing ideas, and an annual 3-day conference for self-publishers.

Appendix D

Cookbook Distributors / Book Reviewers

In addition to contacting both Unique and Quality for library distribution, and Ingram and Baker & Taylor for national distribution (see Chapter Seven), contact the specialty cookbook distributors listed below. Also look through *Literary Market Place*, at your local library, for wholesalers and distributors.

Distributors and Wholesalers

There are several distributors who exclusively handle cookbooks, as well as some major distributors you may be interested in contacting.

The Cookbook Collection is a national distributor for non-profit organizations and self-publishers who have community and specialty cookbooks. Website: www.cookbookstore.com.

Dot Gibson Distributing mails a yearly catalog to 10,000 book buyers, retailers, and consumers. They carry cookbooks from large publishers and individuals, specializing in non-profit cookbooks. They also attend gift and book shows. Send your cookbook for consideration to Dot Gibson, Dot Gibson Distributing, P.O. Box 117, Waycross, GA 31502. 912/285-2848. Website: www.dotgibson.com.

Consortium Book Sales and Distribution, 34 Thirteenth Avenue, Suite 101, Minneapolis, MN 55413. Phone: 612/746-2600. Website: www.cbsd.com.

Independent Publishers Group, 814 North Franklin Street, Chicago, IL 60610. Phone: 312/337-0747. Website: www.ipgbook.com.

Midpoint Trade Books, 27 West 20th Street, Suite 1102, New York, NY 10011. 212/727-0190. www.midpointtradebooks.com.

National Book Network, 4710 University Way, Lanham, MD 20706. Phone: 301/459-3366. Website: www.nbnbooks.com.

Publishers Group West, 1700 Fourth Street, Berkeley, CA 94710. Phone: 510/528-1444. Website: www.pgw.com.

Book Reviewers

Book reviews are an important, integral part of your marketing and promotion plans. The more people who know about your cookbook, the more sales you can make. Send a review copy (or a flyer with a reply card) to anyone involved with food, from newspaper and magazine food editors to teachers at cooking schools and owners of gourmet kitchen boutiques. Book reviews get the word out about your cookbook to the general public and are of vital interest to booksellers and librarians.

The following is a partial list of magazines, newspapers, and major book reviewers. For a more comprehensive list, look in LMP and also contact Bradley Communications to receive a free catalog of media mailing lists. P.O. Box 1206, Lansdowne, PA 19050-8206. Phone: 800/989-1400. Bacon's Information, Inc., publishes print directories and electronic databases of contacts for newspapers, magazines, radio, and television, 332 South Michigan Avenue, Chicago, IL 60604. Phone: 312/922-2400 or 800/621-0561. Additionally, many of the magazines listed in Appendix F do book reviews.

Magazines and Newspapers

In addition to sending your cookbook to appropriate magazines for review, send it to your local paper and the following key newspapers. Also look in LMP under the section Newspapers Featuring Books to find other newspapers that would be appropriate for a review of your cookbook. It's a good idea to call before sending your cookbook to get the correct reviewer's name and title, as editors come and go, and to find out their procedure for submitting a review copy.

Book/Mark Quarterly Review, Mindy Kronenberg, P.O. Box 516, Miller Place, NY 11764. Phone: 631/331-4118. A website is in progress. They publish reviews of books and magazines by small presses and non-corporate publishing entities.

BookPage, ProMotion, Inc., 2143 Belcourt Ave., Nashville, TN 37212. Phone: 615/292-8926. Website: www.bookpage.com. This consumer-oriented newspaper is used by booksellers and libraries to promote new titles and authors.

Chicago Tribune Books, Elizabeth Taylor, Book Review Editor, 435 N. Michigan Avenue, Room 400, Chicago, IL 66011. Phone: 312/222-3232. Website: www.tribune.com.

ForeWord, ForeWord Magazine, Inc., 129-1/2 Front Street, Traverse City, MI 49684. Phone: 231/933-3699. Website: www.forewordmagazine.com. This trade journal for libraries and booksellers reviews new titles from independent publishers and university presses.

Independent Publisher, Jenkins Group, Phil Murphy, 400 West Front Street, Traverse City, MI 49684. Phone: 231/933-0445. Website: www.bookpublishing.com. This magazine reviews small press titles.

Los Angeles Times Book Review, Steve Wasserman, Book Review Editor, 202 West First Street, Los Angeles, CA 90012. Phone: 213/237-7001. Website: www.latimes.com.

New York Review of Books, Barbara Epstein, Editor, 1755 Broadway, 5th Floor, New York, NY 10019. Phone: 212/757-8070. Website: www.nybooks.com. This biweekly tabloid reviews new titles and also prints excerpts—recipes, in your case.

New York Times Book Review, Charles McGrath, 229 West 43rd Street, New York, NY 10036. 212/556-1234. www.nytimes.com. They review cookbooks at Christmas time.

Q B R The Black Book Review, ALEP Inc., 9 West 126th Street, Second Floor, New York, NY 10027. Phone: 212/348-1681. www.qbr.com. This magazine highlights books written by black writers or for a black audience.

San Francisco Chronicle Book Review, Oscar Villalon, Book Review Editor, 901 Mission Street, San Francisco, CA 94103. Phone: 415/777-7043. Website: www.sfgate.com/chronicle.

Small Press Review, Len Fulton, Dustbooks, P.O. Box 100, Paradise, CA 95967. Phone: 530/877-6110. www.dustbooks.com. They feature reviews and news about small presses and magazines.

USA Today, Deirdre Donahue, Book Review Editor, 1000 Wilson Boulevard, Arlington, VA 22209. Phone: 703/276-5494. Website: www.usatoday.com/life/books/front.htm. This newspaper does book reviews and features books in news stories and other articles.

Village Voice Literary Supplement, Joy Press, Editor, 36 Cooper Square, New York, NY 10003. Phone: 212/475-3300. Website: www.villagevoice.com. This monthly newspaper reviews all types of books. Thirty percent of the books they review are cookbooks.

Book World, c/o *The Washington Post*, Marie Arana, Editor, 1150 15th Street, N.W., Washington, DC 20071. Phone: 202/334-7882. Website: www.washingtonpost.com. Currently, they do not review self-published books but this policy may change in the near future.

Since three out of ten women buy cookbooks, it's a good idea to let magazines that women read know about your cookbook. Contact the following magazines about book reviews and/or articles and excerpts.

Better Homes and Gardens, Meredith Corp., 1716 Locust Street, Des Moines, IA 50309-3023. Phone: 515/284-3000. Website: www.bhg.com. Here's a fun fact: *The Better Homes and Gardens New Cookbook* is the third bestselling book in the world, coming in after the Bible and the dictionary.

Family Circle, Meredith Corp., 375 Lexington Avenue, New York, NY 10017. Phone: 212/499-2000. www.familycircle.com.

Good Housekeeping, The Hearst Corp., 250 West 55th Street, New York, NY 10019. 212/499-2200. www.goodhousekeeing.com.

Ladies' Home Journal, Meredith Corp., 125 Park Avenue, 20th Floor, New York, NY 10017. Phone: 212/557-6600. www.lhj.com.

Redbook, The Hearst Corp., 224 West 57th Street, 6th Floor, New York, NY 10019. 212/649-2000. www.redbookmag.com.

Woman's World, Bauer Publishing Co., 270 Sylvan Avenue, Englewood Cliffs, NJ 07632. Phone: 201/569-6699.

Major Book Reviewers

These are the biggies. Getting your cookbook reviewed by a major book reviewer will have a huge impact on sales, both to bookstores and libraries. They require a prepublication copy, six months in advance of your pub date, which is called bound galleys and is also referred to as an uncorrected page proof. You can create a POD (print on demand) version of your cookbook at www.lulu.com, which looks professional and is reasonably priced, or at your local printer or Kinko's.

On the cover, which is usually plain—if your cover art is ready, put it on your prepub review copy—make it clear that this is a prepub review copy, an uncorrected page proof. If they review your cookbook, the reviews will coincide with your pub date. Show all the vital information—ISBN, pub date, author, publisher, binding, distributor, list price, book size, and other relevant information on the back cover.

Booklist, Brad Hooper, American Library Association, 50 East Huron Street, Chicago, IL 60611. Phone: 800/545-2433. Website: www.ala.org/booklist.

Kirkus Reviews, 770 Broadway, 6th Floor, New York, NY 10003. Phone: 646/654-5000 or 646/654-4602. Website: www.kirkusreviews.com.

Library Journal, Book Review Editor, 360 Park Avenue, South, New York, NY 10010. 888/800-5473. www.libraryjournal.com.

Midwest Book Review, James Cox, Editor, 278 Orchard Drive, Oregon, WI 53575. Phone: 608/835-7937. www.midwestbookreview.com.

Publishers Weekly, 360 Park Avenue South, New York, NY 10010. Phone: 646/746-6758. Website: www.publishersweekly.com.

Appendix E

Recommended Reading List

The following list of reference books about writing, finding a publisher or agent, and publishing, offers a brief description of each book.

Reference Books

Literary Market Place, published annually by R. R. Bowker, is a comprehensive list of everyone in the publishing industry. It also lists printers, freelance editors, cover designers, book clubs, book reviewers, wholesalers and distributors, writer's conferences, book trade events, awards, and much more.

The Recipe Writer's Handbook, published by Wiley, offers lots of information on writing recipes but is a bit difficult to find; you may have to special order it from a bookstore.

Will Write for Food, published by Marlowe and Company, offers a guide to writing cookbooks, restaurant reviews, food articles, memoir, fiction, and more.

Jeff Herman's Guide to Book Publishers, Editors, & Literary Agents, published by Three Dog Press, offers a comprehensive list of editors and agents along with a personality profile and the type of books they're interested in receiving.

The Writer's Handbook, published annually by The Writer Books, lists book publishers, agents, conferences, and includes articles on writing and publishing.

Writer's Market, published annually by Writer's Digest Books, is the premier reference book to help you find publishers who are suitable for your book. It has detailed listings, including the name of the acquiring editor, royalty information, and submission requirements. It includes a small listing of agents and contains articles about writing and publishing.

Writer's Digest Books also publishes *Writer's Market Guide to Literary Agents*. This annual volume can help you locate an agent to represent your cookbook.

The Path to Publishing Your Book, Gloria Chadwick, Riverstone Publishing. Guides writers from beginning to end—all the way through writing their book, putting together a perfect proposal, negotiating a book contract, and seeing their book on the bookstore shelf. Packed full of encouragement, ideas, and inspiration to get writers going and keep them moving, it's a helpful how-to.

Books on Self-Publishing, Marketing, and Promotion

The authors of the following books provide publishing and marketing information and services that supplement their books.

The Complete Guide to Book Marketing, David Cole, Allworth Press. Offers great information, ideas, and resources for marketing your book. David Cole is a marketing consultant with Gemini Marketing and Communications. 510/526-2916. www.gemcole.com.

The Complete Guide to Self-Publishing, Tom & Marilyn Ross, Writer's Digest Books. Offers everything you need to know about self-publishing, marketing, and promoting your book. Marilyn Ross offers phone consultation and on-going book coaching for self-published authors. 719/395-8659. www.selfpublishingresources.com.

How to Make Big Profits Publishing City & Regional Books: A Guide for Entrepreneurs, Writers and Publishers, Marilyn & Tom Ross, Communication Creativity. Loads of ideas and techniques for promoting your book. Website: www.communicationcreativity.com.

Jump Start Your Book Sales: A Money-Making Guide for Authors, Independent Publishers and Small Presses, Tom & Marilyn Ross, Communication Creativity. Great advice on the ins and outs of marketing your book. Website: www.communicationcreativity.com.

1001 Ways to Market Your Books for Authors and Publishers, John Kremer, Open Horizons. As the title implies, there are 1001 ways to sell your book. This book provides numerous contacts and leads. It's updated every few years. Be sure to get the latest edition.

John Kremer offers many marketing and publicity kits. Open Horizons, P.O. Box 205, Fairfield, IA 52556. Phone: 800/796-6130. Website: www.bookmarket.com.

Publish to Win: Smart Strategies to Sell More Books, Jerrold Jenkins and Anne Stanton, Rhodes & Easton. This book offers a plethora of ideas and resources that any writer will find valuable. Contact The Jenkins Group, 121 East Front Street, Traverse City, MI 49684 for additional services provided to self-publishers, including book exhibits. 800/706-4636. Website: www.bookpublishing.com.

The Self-Publishing Manual, Dan Poynter, Para Publishing. Offers solid information, from idea inception to publishing and promoting. It is updated every few years. Be sure to get the latest edition. Dan Poynter offers a self-publishing seminar and marketing reports. Para Publishing, P.O. Box 8206-890, Santa Barbara, CA 93118-8206. Phone: 800/727-2782. Website: www.parapublishing.com.

Appendix F

Food Magazines

A list of food magazines, with information on how to contact them to either write for them, submit a recipe, subscribe, or send your cookbook for review, follows. Their websites also have great recipes. It's a good idea to read several issues to see the magazine's style, the type of writing that will fit their needs, and how your recipes and cookbook will fit in.

Bon Appetit covers culinary diversity by highlighting restaurants, chefs, and regional cuisines. Departments include quick menus, healthful cooking, and what's new in the marketplace. Condé Nast Publications, Inc., 6300 Wilshire Blvd., Floor 10, Los Angeles, CA 90048. Phone: 323/965-3600. Website: www.bonappetit.com.

Chile Pepper features peppers and zesty cuisine. It includes recipes and information on Southwestern foods, Caribbean cooking, Asian cuisine, Mid-Eastern, Cajun, and more. 110 Williams Street, 23rd Floor, New York, NY 10038. Phone: 646/459-4800. Website: www.chilepepper.com.

Chocolatier focuses on the preparation and presentation of elegant desserts featuring creations from professional chefs and its own test kitchens, providing instructions to recreate them at home. 45 West 34th Street, Suite 600, New York, NY 10001. Phone: 212/239-0855. Website: www.godiva.com.

Cook's Illustrated offers articles on the techniques of home cooking and features recipes based on careful testing. Boston Common Press, 17 Station Street, Brookline, MA 02445, Phone: 617/232-1000. Website: www.cooksillustrated.com.

Cooking Light focuses on eating smart and being fit. P.O. Box 62376, Tampa, FL 33662. Website: www.cookinglight.com.

Cooking Pleasures is for people who are passionate about food and cooking. It provides new recipes and techniques. Topics range from ethnic foods to everyday meals, with an emphasis on scratch cooking, using readily available ingredients. It features member recipes, tips, questions, and food testing. www.cookingclub.com.

Fancy Food & Culinary Products covers specialty foods, natural foods, confections and housewares. 20 West Kinzie, 12th Floor, Chicago, IL 60610. Phone: 312/849-2200. Website: www.talcott.com.

Fine Cooking is for people who love to cook. The focus is on giving readers useful advice to get the best results from the recipes. Departments include international cuisines, quick cooking, equipment, wines, and food science. www.taunton.com/finecooking.

Food and Wine celebrates various aspects of the epicurean lifestyle. American Express Publishing Corp., 1120 Avenue of the Americas, 9th Floor, New York, NY 10036. Phone: 212/382-5600. www.foodandwine.com.

Gourmet covers subjects from food and travel to cooking, restaurants, and entertaining. Condé Nast Publications, Inc., 4 Times Square, 5th Floor, New York, NY 10036. Phone: 212/286-2860. www.gourmet.com.

Kashrus provides up-to-date information to the kosher consumer on food, travel, catering, health issues, mislabeled food products, and more. P.O. Box 204, Brooklyn, NY 11204. Phone: 718/336-8544. Website: www.kashrusmagazine.com.

Northwest Palate covers food, wine, and travel in the Pacific Northwest. P.O. Box 10860, Portland, OR 97296. Phone: 503/224-6039. Website: www.nwpalate.com.

Saveur is for people who are passionate about food, drink, travel, and adventure. Website: www.saveur.com.

Vegetarian Times presents the latest scientific research. Sabot Publishing, Inc., 301 Concourse Blvd., Suite 350, Glen Allen, VA 23059. Phone: 804/346-0990. Website: www.vegetariantimes.com.

Veggie Life is for people interested in low-fat, meatless cuisine and nutrition. EWG Publishing Co., 1041 Shary Circle, Concord, CA 94518. Phone: 925/671-9852. Website: www.veggielife.com.

Appendix G

Sample Query Letter and Cookbook
Proposal for *Food & Flavors of San Antonio*

The following query letter and cookbook proposal offers a guideline in putting together a cookbook proposal to submit to a commercial publisher. Vary the format to fit the style and theme of your cookbook. Sample recipes that were submitted with the proposal are not included, but since there's extra space on this page, here's a great recipe:

Red Rice and Beans

Rice and beans are served with almost everything in San Antonio. Sometimes they're mixed together, as in this recipe; other times they're served side-by-side on a combination plate with guacamole, chopped lettuce, and tomatoes on the side.

1 cup tomato juice
1/2 tsp. garlic powder
1/8 tsp. cayenne pepper
1/4 tsp. cumin
1 (15.5 oz.) can dark red kidney beans,
   rinsed, drained, and slightly mashed
3 cups hot, cooked white rice

In a medium-size saucepan, heat the tomato juice, garlic powder, cayenne pepper, cumin, and beans to boiling. Stir to mix.

Reduce the heat to low. Cover and cook for 5 minutes, stirring occasionally.

Stir in the cooked rice and heat through.

**Gloria Chadwick 📖 Address
Phone 📖 email 📖 Website**

Current Date

Editor's Name and Title
Publisher Name
Address
City / State / Zip

Dear Editor's Name:

Foods & Flavors of San Antonio offers the foods and flavors of the
Tex-Mex capital of the world. The 300 recipes, some from San Antonio
restaurants specializing in Southwest fare, some from local celebrities,
some from down home cooks, and some of my own share the tastes of
San Antonio. The cookbook contains an armchair tour of the attractions
interspersed with the recipes in each section. There is supplementary
information about food festivals and fiestas, a glossary of chile peppers,
and a resource guide.

In addition to being the author of 18 books, including 4 self-published
cookbooks, I've studied culinary arts, worked in several restaurants, and
been a gourmet cook and foodie for 34 years. Previously published books
include: *Discovering Your Past Lives*, 1988, *Spirituality & Self-Empowerment*, 1995, both by Contemporary Books, *Reincarnation and Your Past
Life Memories*, 1999, Random House, *Inner Journeys*, 2006, Llewellyn,
The Path to Publishing Your Book, 2007, Riverstone Publishing, *Future
Lives*, 2008, Sterling, and *The Complete Do-it-Yourself Guide to Past
Life Regression*, forthcoming, Sterling.

The cookbook will appeal to everyone who enjoys Tex-Mex food, as
well as to the 1,592,986 residents of San Antonio, and especially to the
2.5 million visitors per year. Additionally, I can sell the book through various markets and connections I have established through promoting my
other cookbooks.

Enclosed is a proposal for your consideration. I'm looking forward to
hearing from you and have included a SASE for your reply.

Very sincerely,

Gloria Chadwick

GS/s
Enclosures

Foods & Flavors of San Antonio

© 2007 by Gloria Chadwick

Address

Phone Number

email

Website

Approximate Page Count — 230

Foods & Flavors of San Antonio

Proposal Contents

Overview

Foods & Flavors of San Antonio offers Southwest cooking from
the heart of San Antonio. The foods include 300 recipes—some
from Mexican restaurants, local celebrities, down home cooks, and
some of my own. The flavors present the sights, attractions, and
fiestas of the Tex-Mex capital of the world.

Inside this combination cookbook/tour guide, you'll find:

- A rich tapestry of the history and local flavor of San Antonio:
  The Alamo, HemisFair '68, the San Antonio Chili Queens,
  and much more;

- Tourist treats: Places to go, things to do and see, and a
  comprehensive calendar of events which includes fiestas
  and local festivals; and

- A glossary of chile peppers and a resource guide.

This cookbook brings the essence of San Antonio into your kitchen,
no matter where you live. It's a perfect keepsake for tourists and is a
must in every San Antonio kitchen.

Author Bio

Gloria Chadwick is the author of eighteen books, including *Discovering Your Past Lives*, 1988, *Spirituality and Self-Empowerment*, 1995, both published by Contemporary Books, *Somewhere Over the Rainbow*, 1992, *Life is Just a Dream*, 1998, *Happy Ways to Heal the Earth*, 1999, *Soul Shimmers*, 2000, Mystical Mindscapes, *Reincarnation and Your Past-Life Memories*, 1999, Random House, *Inner Journeys*, 2006, Llewellyn, *The Path to Publishing Your Book*, 2007, Riverstone Publishing, *Future Lives*, 2008, Sterling Publishing, and *The Complete Do-it-Yourself Guide to Past Life Regression*, forthcoming, Sterling.

She is also the author of four self-published cookbooks: *Really Good Recipes*, 2000, *Food Feasts*, 2001, *Best of the Barbecues*, 2002, and *The Cheapie Chicken Cookbook*, 2003. She has recently completed *Recipe for a Cookbook: How to Write, Publish, and Promote Your Cookbook*.

She studied culinary arts, worked in several restaurants, and has been a gourmet cook and foodie for thirty-four years. She moved to San Antonio two years ago and began exploring the city to see and sample all the sights and foods it has to offer. This inspired *Foods & Flavors of San Antonio*.

Table of Contents with Chapter Summaries

Introduction — Tex-Mex Tour

An introductory tour through the foods, flavors, and flair that makes San Antonio the Tex-Mex capital of the world.

Appetizers

If you like flowers, visit the Botanical Gardens or the Japanese Tea Garden. *Meaty Nachos* or *Guacamole Cheese Chips* are sure to please. *Tomatillo Salsa* served with tortilla chips is a great beginning to any meal or for a snack. (19 recipes)

Beverages

Visit the water gardens at HemisFair Park. For the more adventurous, go tubing on the Guadalupe River in nearby New Braunfels. *Cool Kahlua* or *Texas Tea* are refreshing on hot, sunny days. *Tequila Sunrise* or a *Margarita* are two of the favorite drinks in San Antonio. (14 recipes)

Breakfast

Visit the San Jose Mission, one of the four missions that comprise Mission Trail. Listen to the mariachis play on Sunday morning. San Antonians start their morning with a breakfast of eggs and salsa, wrapped up in tortillas. *Eggs Olé* is a bright beginning to a sun-filled day. *Huevos Ranchero* is definitely an eye-opener. (15 recipes)

Salads

Walk through La Villita to see local artists who display and sell their colorful artwork. *South of the Border Salad* makes a meal all by itself. *Grilled Chicken Strip Salad* easily turns into a wrap for a light lunch. (11 recipes)

Soups & Stews

Visit Market Square, also known as El Mercado. Browse through the numerous specialty shops and sidewalk vendors. Enjoy the flavor of San Antonio. *Chicken Chiles 'n Corn Soup* is spiced with flavor. *Green Chile Pork Stew* is great for either lunch or dinner. (25 recipes)

Veggies, Rice & Beans

If you're in San Antonio during Fiesta, be sure to attend NIOSA: Night in Old San Antonio. Rice and beans are a staple in San Antonio. Charro or refried beans are on almost every plate. *Fiesta Rice* sets a festive mood for your meal. *Chuckwagon Corn* will complement any dinner. (44 recipes)

Sandwiches, Tacos & Fajitas

Stroll along the River Walk or take a boat tour on the San Antonio River. Enjoy lunch at one of the outdoor cafes. Tacos are traditional in San Antonio. Fajitas, burritos, enchiladas, and quesadillas round out the lunch menu. (27 recipes)

Chili

Remember the Alamo. How could you forget when San Antonio is the chili capital of the world. *Beer 'n Black Bean Chili* and *Corn Chip Chili* will prove it. The prize-winning recipe from the 2004 Chili Cook-off in Terlingua is included. (20 recipes)

Beef and Pork

The Texas Folklife Festival, held annually in June on the fairgrounds of the Institute of Texan Cultures, reflects the cultures, food, and lifestyles that make up San Antonio. From *Alamo City Pot Roast* to *Tex-Mex Pork Tenderloin*, you'll feast on mouth-watering dinners. (36 recipes)

Chicken

If shopping is your style, visit RiverCenter Mall, the North Star Mall with the giant cowboy boots, the Shops at La Cantera, or head over to the outdoor Quarry Market with the huge smokestacks. *Chicken Olé* and *Chicken Fiesta* are seasoned in true Southwest style. (32 recipes)

Seafood

If you like basketball, you'll enjoy watching the San Antonio Spurs play at the SBC Center. The nearby gulf cities provide fresh fish. *Texas Garlic Shrimp, Corpus Christi Crab Cakes,* and *San Antonio Sole* are the best in town. (8 recipes)

Breads & Tortillas

Go 600 feet up to the top of the Tower of the Americas, built for HemisFair '68, San Antonio's World's Fair, and enjoy the view of the city. You'll want lots of *Cheesy Chile Corn Bread* or *Homemade Tortillas* to go with your bowl of red or to sop up all the flavorful sauces. (10 recipes)

Salsas, Sauces & Seasonings

Take the kids to the San Antonio Zoo, visit the cultural and kid-friendly Witte Museum, or attend a rodeo and see Texas cowboys. Sauces and southwest seasonings enhance and cover your meals, San Antonio style. (18 recipes)

Sweets & Treats

Attend the Poteet Strawberry Festival in April, just outside of San Antonio for strawberry treats and a carnival. *Kahlua Cheesecake* is a wonderfully rich way to end a meal. *Pecan Pie* is a tradition. (14 recipes)

Resource Guides

Chile Peppers. What they are, how to use them, and where to buy them.

Calendar of Events. A list of fiestas and festivals, with dates and contact information.

Index

Competition

Savor the Southwest, Barbara Fenzl, Bay Books, 1999. This cookbook focuses on Southwest cooking in Arizona, New Mexico, Texas, California, and Colorado with recipes from restaurant chefs. My cookbook focuses on San Antonio cooking with local recipes from restaurants, celebrities, and down home cooks.

Jane Butel's Tex-Mex Cookbook, Jane Butel, Three Rivers Press, 1980. The author's recipes are Santa Fe-specific. Mine are San Antonio-specific.

The Everything Mexican Cookbook, Margaret Kaeter, Adams Media, 2004. This cookbook focuses on Mexican food, as the title states. The 300 recipes are rather generic and aren't especially appealing or appetizing. Many of the recipes call for separate recipes that must be prepared to include in specific recipes. This isn't user-friendly.

Rick Bayless's Mexican Kitchen, Rick Bayless, Scribner, 1996. Rick Bayless is an expert on Mexican food. However, his recipes call for unfamiliar ingredients that are difficult to come by, i.e., huitlacoche, epazote leaves, hoja santa, to name a few. His other cookbooks are similar. My cookbook focuses on foods that people eat in San Antonio and features ingredients which are easy to find and recipes that are easy to prepare.

The Tex-Mex Cookbook, Robb Walsh, Broadway Books, 2004. This cookbook offers a variety of Tex-Mex recipes, along with interesting information about the origins of the recipes. While there are several anecdotes and references to San Antonio, this cookbook covers all regions of Tex-Mex cooking.

The Very Best of Tex-Mex Cooking, Jim Peyton, Maverick Publishing Company, 2005. This cookbook offers well-researched history on Texas cooking and authentic recipes. While the cover shows the Alamo, there is only a brief mention of San Antonio style cooking.

The next two cookbooks are the most direct competition. They are focused on San Antonio food, as is my cookbook.

Los Barrios Family Cookbook, Diana Barrios Treviño, Villard Books, 2002. This cookbook focuses on the family recipes which are served in the Los Barrios restaurant in San Antonio. Much of the commentary is devoted to family history and memories.

Celebrate San Antonio, San Antonio Junior Forum, Wimmer Cookbooks (self-published), 1986. This cookbook has been selling for more than 20 years; this is a tribute to the popularity of the foods of San Antonio. It mentions a few tourist attractions but doesn't give contact information. There are several errors including repeated pages and a few of the recipes have missing ingredients, i.e., a recipe for lamb kebobs calls for a marinade and tells readers to check the index but the marinade isn't listed. Most of the recipes are from home cooks; the recipes from local chefs feature Italian, German, and French cuisine, along with some Southwest recipes. My cookbook focuses on Southwest food prepared and served in San Antonio, and provides the local history and tourist attractions with contact information.

Foods & Flavors of San Antonio offers 300 authentic San Antonio recipes. This cookbook offers more than recipes; it offers a commentary of the rich history and local lore, along with a calendar of fiestas and an armchair tour of the sights in San Antonio. The recipes allow cooks everywhere to prepare San Antonio style meals just like they'd enjoy if they were eating in San Antonio.

Marketing / Promotion

Previous media coverage includes radio talk shows, cable TV appearances, newspaper articles and interviews, and book signings. I can use all these avenues to promote my book.

Several prominent chefs and cookbook authors may write endorsements for the book.

• Chef David Miller, my culinary arts teacher, owner of Chef by Request, a Chicago catering service, and Kafe Kokopelli, a restaurant featuring Southwest fare. Additionally, he will offer this cookbook in his restaurant, to students in his culinary arts classes, to his clients (650+), and through the Association of Culinary Professionals mailing list (25,000).

• Rick Bayless, chef and author of *Mexico: One Plate at a Time* and several other Mexican cookbooks. Chef David Miller is a personal friend and will ask Rick for an endorsement.

• Diana Barrios Treviño, author of *Los Barrios Family Cookbook*. Even though my cookbook will be competing with hers, she may be willing to offer an endorsement, as she did for the following cookbook author.

• Jim Peyton, author of *The Very Best of Tex-Mex Cooking*. I met him at a book signing and we discussed this cookbook. He is willing to write an endorsement.

In addition to being sold in bookstores nationwide, this cookbook will sell very well in the souvenir shop at the Alamo, as well as other tourist attractions and wherever San Antonio souvenirs are sold.

The numerous gift shops and boutiques in nearby Fredericksburg, Texas, might be interested in carrying the cookbook.

The Good Cook Book Club may want to feature this cookbook. Additionally, it can be showcased in numerous cookbook catalogs.

The chefs, celebrities, and local media who contribute to this cookbook are a built-in market. The chefs may be willing to sell the cookbook in their restaurants and the media may help promote it in other ways.

Press releases could be sent and followed up with ads or excerpts placed in the food section of newspapers and food magazines. Perhaps they would print a recipe or do an article.

I rent a booth at many local book fairs and community festivals every year; I can sell the book there. Fiesta Week attracts millions of residents and tourists.

The Crossroads Mall in San Antonio has a Sample the Southwest weekend in November. I can rent a booth there to sell the cookbook.

Perhaps we could also offer the cookbook at the taco breakfast at Crossroads Mall.

I can promote the cookbook extensively on my website and on other sites on the Internet.

I've done several signings at the local Barnes & Noble. They are receptive to setting up a launch party for this cookbook and have agreed to showcase and hand-sell it. Additionally, I will approach other local bookstores to arrange book signings.

Libraries and other organizations might be interested in sponsoring a talk about writing this cookbook with back-of-the-room book sales.

Local TV stations may be interested in doing an interview or a segment about the cookbook. Great Day, SA would be a good show to approach.

San Antonio College sponsors an annual book fair the first weekend in April. I can sell the cookbook there.

The Texas Book Festival in Austin, held in November, would be a good place to showcase and sell the cookbook.

I can have postcards or recipe cards with the cookbook information printed to give to grocery stores for them to put in every customer's bag. Perhaps they'd also carry the cookbook.

We can ask the Visitor's Information Bureau to put a flyer about the cookbook in their information packet. We could also produce a pamphlet to place at all the tourist attractions.

Perhaps the city of San Antonio will adopt this cookbook as its official cookbook.

Market Square, an enclosed mall which spills out into an open-air market, catering to the tourist trade, has more than 100 stores and sidewalk vendors featuring the foods and flavors of San Antonio. One store is devoted exclusively to southwest spices and carries cookbooks. They might be interested in carrying mine.

Other retail stores may want to carry the cookbook. All the local Wal-Mart stores have a section specifically for Texas souvenirs. We could place the cookbook in all these places.

Several instructors who teach cooking classes in the continuing education program where I teach are willing to feature recipes and offer the book in their classes.

Food and Leisure magazine did a four-page article on the *Los Barrios Family Cookbook*; perhaps they would do an article on my cookbook.

We could place ads in the tourist magazines which are distributed free in hundreds of locations to tourists.

There is also a coupon book for tourist attractions, merchandise, and restaurants; perhaps we could place a coupon offering a dollar or two off the retail price.

I will approach the managers of San Antonio hotels and extended stay suites and ask them to offer my cookbook for sale to their guests.

Along those same lines, I will contact Realtors and large apartment complexes, to inquire if they'd like to buy the cookbook as a premium to give as a gift to new home buyers and renters. Banks may also be interested in a premium purchase.

I have friends and family in several states—Illinois, Colorado, California, Florida, and Maryland—who are willing to help promote this cookbook by approaching bookstores and retail stores in their area with a sell sheet. They've helped me promote all my other cookbooks in this manner.

Many schools, churches, and organizations in the San Antonio area that support charitable causes might buy quantities of the cookbook as a fundraiser.

The cookbook can be sold on a website for products produced by Texas residents at www.texascapitolgiftshop.com.

Book Specs

The cookbook will contain 300 recipes, short anecdotes about the contributing chefs and their restaurants, and blurbs about local celebrities (some Spurs). There is an armchair tour of attractions interspersed with the recipes (a thumbnail sketch is included with this proposal). It will include a calendar of fiestas and food festivals, a glossary of chile peppers, a resource guide, and an index. The approximate page count is 230.

Cover Suggestion: A colorful collage of Tex-Mex food and some of the major attractions, such as the Alamo, the Tower of the Americas, and the River Walk.

Foods & Flavors of San Antonio is half complete; it can be finished within six months. I can supply both a hard copy and a disk (Dell PC, Microsoft Word).

Index